# Office of Juvenile Justice and Delinquency Prevention

The Office of Juvenile Justice and Delinquency Prevention (OJJDP) was established by the President and Congress through the Juvenile Justice and Delinquency Prevention (JJDP) Act of 1974, Public Law 93–415, as amended. Located within the Office of Justice Programs of the U.S. Department of Justice, OJJDP's goal is to provide national leadership in addressing the issues of juvenile delinquency and improving juvenile justice.

OJJDP sponsors a broad array of research, program, and training initiatives to improve the juvenile justice system as a whole, as well as to benefit individual youth-serving agencies. These initiatives are carried out by seven components within OJJDP, described below.

**Research and Program Development Division** develops knowledge on national trends in juvenile delinquency; supports a program for data collection and information sharing that incorporates elements of statistical and systems development; identifies how delinquency develops and the best methods for its prevention, intervention, and treatment; and analyzes practices and trends in the juvenile justice system.

**Training and Technical Assistance Division** provides juvenile justice training and technical assistance to Federal, State, and local governments; law enforcement, judiciary, and corrections personnel; and private agencies, educational institutions, and community organizations.

**Special Emphasis Division** provides discretionary funds to public and private agencies, organizations, and individuals to replicate tested approaches to delinquency prevention, treatment, and control in such pertinent areas as chronic juvenile offenders, community-based sanctions, and the disproportionate representation of minorities in the juvenile justice system.

**State Relations and Assistance Division** supports collaborative efforts by States to carry out the mandates of the JJDP Act by providing formula grant funds to States; furnishing technical assistance to States, local governments, and private agencies; and monitoring State compliance with the JJDP Act.

**Information Dissemination Unit** produces and distributes information resources on juvenile justice research, training, and programs and coordinates the Office's program planning and competitive award activities. Information that meets the needs of juvenile justice professionals and policymakers is provided through print and online publications, videotapes, CD–ROM's, electronic listservs, and the Office's Web site. As part of the program planning and award process, IDU develops priorities, publishes solicitations and application kits for funding opportunities, and facilitates the peer review process for discretionary funding awards.

**Concentration of Federal Efforts Program** promotes interagency cooperation and coordination among Federal agencies with responsibilities in the area of juvenile justice. The Program primarily carries out this responsibility through the Coordinating Council on Juvenile Justice and Delinquency Prevention, an independent body within the executive branch that was established by Congress through the JJDP Act.

**Child Protection Division** administers programs related to crimes against children and children's exposure to violence. The Division provides leadership and funding to promote effective policies and procedures to address the problems of missing and exploited children, children who have been abused or neglected, and children exposed to domestic or community violence. CPD program activities include conducting research; providing information, training, and technical assistance on programs to prevent and respond to child victims, witnesses, and their families; developing and demonstrating effective child protection initiatives; and supporting the National Center for Missing and Exploited Children.

The mission of OJJDP is to provide national leadership, coordination, and resources to prevent and respond to juvenile offending and child victimization. OJJDP accomplishes its mission by supporting States, local communities, and tribal jurisdictions in their efforts to develop and implement effective, multidisciplinary prevention and intervention programs and improve the capacity of the juvenile justice system to protect public safety, hold offenders accountable, and provide treatment and rehabilitative services tailored to the needs of individual juveniles and their families.

# Safe From the Start:
# Taking Action on Children
# Exposed to Violence

## Summary

**John J. Wilson, Acting Administrator**
Office of Juvenile Justice and Delinquency Prevention

November 2000

**U.S. Department of Justice**
**Office of Justice Programs**
**Office of Juvenile Justice and Delinquency Prevention**
810 Seventh Street NW.
Washington, DC 20531

**Janet Reno**
*Attorney General*

**Daniel Marcus**
*Acting Associate Attorney General*

**Mary Lou Leary**
*Acting Assistant Attorney General*

**John J. Wilson**
*Acting Administrator*
Office of Juvenile Justice and Delinquency Prevention

This document was prepared for the U.S. Departments of Justice and Health and Human Services by Wendy B. Jacobson.

Points of view or opinions expressed in this document are those of the author and do not necessarily represent the official position or policies of OJJDP or the U.S. Department of Justice.

The Office of Juvenile Justice and Delinquency Prevention is a component of the Office of Justice Programs, which also includes the Bureau of Justice Assistance, the Bureau of Justice Statistics, the National Institute of Justice, and the Office for Victims of Crime.

*On June 22, 1999, Attorney General Janet Reno and Secretary of Health and Human Services Donna E. Shalala, with the leadership of Deputy Attorney General Eric Holder, brought together 150 practitioners and policymakers in a National Summit on preventing and reducing the negative impact of children's exposure to violence. This blueprint for Federal, State, and local action is the product of their commitment, energy, and expertise.*

# Foreword

The prevalence of violence in our communities, neighborhoods, and homes places children at high risk of exposure.

The potential for harm to children exposed to violence is considerable. In the short term, children's lives are often radically disrupted when their parents, loved ones, or they themselves are harmed. A range of feelings is evoked, including helplessness, hopelessness, fear, and aggression, among others.

The long-term effects can be devastating, including difficulties in school, work, and relationships and physical and mental health problems. Children exposed to violence may be revictimized later in life, or they may become victimizers themselves, as studies indicate that children exposed to violence are at greater risk of perpetrating violent acts.

Convened by the U.S. Departments of Justice and Health and Human Services, the National Summit on Children Exposed to Violence brought experts together to develop a framework for understanding and addressing children's exposure to violence. This Summary describes that framework, creating an action plan that outlines principles for preventing and reducing the negative impact of the exposure to violence on children.

Through understanding the challenges, knowing the facts, constructing effective programs, and working across disciplines, we are taking a significant step toward ensuring a safe start for all children.

**John J. Wilson**
*Acting Administrator*
Office of Juvenile Justice and Delinquency Prevention

# Acknowledgments

The U.S. Departments of Justice and Health and Human Services would like to thank the following individuals and organizations, whose representatives dedicated their time and energy to creating the National Summit on Children Exposed to Violence:

American Bar Association

Child Welfare League of America

Children's Hospital of San Diego

Children's Mental Health Alliance Foundation

CIVITAS Initiative

U.S. Congressman Bud Cramer and Staff

Families and Work Institute

Hayes, Domenici and Associates

I Am Your Child Foundation

Menninger Clinic

Nathan Cummings Foundation

National Children's Alliance

National Council of Juvenile and Family Court Judges

Yale Child Study Center

Unless otherwise noted, quotations in this Action Plan are from Summit participants or from the following three documents that were released at the Summit and whose development was instrumental to its success:

*Effective Intervention in Domestic Violence and Child Maltreatment Cases: Guidelines for Policy and Practice,* recommendations from the National Council of Juvenile and Family Court Judges, 1999.

*Breaking the Cycle of Violence: Recommendations To Improve the Criminal Justice Response to Child Victims and Witnesses,* U.S. Department of Justice, Office of Justice Programs, Office for Victims of Crime, Monograph, June 1999, NCJ 176983 (for availability information, see p. x).

*Children Exposed to Violence: Recommendations for State Justice Systems,* U.S. Department of Justice, Office of the Deputy Attorney General, 1999, NCJ 180494 (for availability information, see p. x).

Additional quotations are from *Through My Eyes*, NCJ 178229, a video about children's exposure to violence, also produced for the Summit (for availability information, see p. x).

# Table of Contents

This Action Plan contains information on resources available to address the issue of children's exposure to violence, including many publications from the U.S. Department of Justice (DOJ). All DOJ publications cited in this Action Plan are available from the National Criminal Justice Reference Service (NCJRS). Most DOJ publications may be downloaded from the NCJRS Justice Information Center Web site at www.ncjrs.org. All DOJ publications may be ordered from NCJRS by mail, phone, or fax, or online, as follows:

**Mail:**      NCJRS Publication Orders
P.O. Box 6000
Rockville, MD 20849–6000

**Telephone:**      800–851–3420

**Fax:**      410–792–4358

**Online:**      www.ncjrs.org/puborder

When ordering by telephone or online, use the National Criminal Justice (NCJ) reference number noted at the end of the publication citation in the text of the Action Plan.

# Executive Summary

The likelihood that today's children will be exposed to some form of violence—in the streets, at school, at home, or in the media—is enormous. In the short term, exposure to violence can result in the total upheaval of a child's life. In the long term, many children exposed to violence experience difficulties in school, at work, and in relationships; have physical and mental health problems; and may be at risk of being revictimized by violence throughout their lives. Additionally, these children are at greater risk of becoming offenders themselves.

Recognizing that today the Nation is facing the consequences of previous inadequate investments to protect its children, the U.S. Departments of Justice (DOJ) and Health and Human Services (HHS) convened a summit of 150 practitioners and policymakers in June 1999 to contemplate the problem of children's exposure to violence and create a national blueprint for action. Professionals from both the public and private sectors joined together, representing child protective services; domestic violence services and advocacy; juvenile and family courts; law enforcement and prosecution; mental health, substance abuse, and healthcare services; family violence prevention services; childhood education and services; and State legislatures. Members of the National Advisory Council on Violence Against Women were also present.

The National Summit on Children Exposed to Violence provided the opportunity to learn from participants' experience and expertise, crafting a set of key operating principles and concrete steps: a practical action agenda. The Action Plan presented in this document describes that agenda, integrating the most up-to-date data on children exposed to violence with the key elements of known best practices, suggesting both discipline-specific and general action steps, and identifying resources for additional information.

## A framework for understanding and addressing children's exposure to violence

The Action Plan recommends that efforts to address children's exposure to violence:

- Reflect a commitment to common goals.

- Be grounded in a full understanding of the issues and challenges involved.

- Be based in fact.

- Fully integrate prevention, intervention, and accountability measures.

- Work across disciplines.

## Committing to common goals

The first step in addressing the problem of children's exposure to violence is commitment to a vision for the future—a vision that includes clear goals and a path for achieving them. Critical to that process is a willingness to consider doing things differently. For policymakers, this means increasing resources for prevention programs and other services at the front end of the system. For justice system professionals, it means being sensitive to the serious impact of violence and victimization on children. For service providers, it means recognizing and building on the strengths of battered women and helping them develop safety strategies for themselves and their children, consistently viewing children within the context of family, and developing comprehensive services that work together. Finally, there must be a commitment from professionals to keep children and their voices at the core of the work that is done on their behalf.

## Understanding the challenges

There are many reasons why successfully responding to the issue of children's exposure to violence has been so difficult and why a clearer understanding of the issue and some basic operating principles around which to organize the work are so critical. Among these reasons are the following:

- **It is a complicated issue.** Children's exposure to violence—how and why it happens, what its consequences are, and what to do about it—is a complicated, multifaceted issue, made even more complex by the steady stream of new data and information. This complexity makes it difficult to agree upon joint strategies.

- **It is a problem people try to avoid.** Denial, discomfort, refusal to identify perpetrators, and "burnout" contribute to the Nation's reluctance to do something about the large numbers of children harmed by violence.

- **It is an issue that divides professionals.** Too often, professionals working with children exposed to violence work in isolation from each other or, worse, at cross-purposes.

## Knowing the facts

Effective strategies for addressing children's exposure to violence must be based on a thorough understanding of the facts surrounding the problem. For example:

**Millions of children are exposed to violence each year.** National estimates based on a 1995 survey indicate that of the Nation's 22.3 million children between the ages of 12 and 17, approximately 1.8 million have been victims of a serious sexual assault, 3.9 million have been victims of a serious physical assault, and almost 9 million have witnessed serious violence. Every day in 1997, six young people (under the age of 18) were murdered; 56 percent of the victims were killed with a firearm.

**Young children are particularly at risk.** Children younger than age 4 accounted for 76 percent of child abuse and neglect fatalities in 1997. Child abuse is the leading cause of death in children under age 1.

**The maltreatment of children and violence against women often go hand in hand.** As many as half a million children may be encountered by police during domestic violence arrests. There is an overlap of 30 to 60 percent between violence against children and violence against women in the same families.

**The home can be a dangerous place.** Far more children are victims of serious physical abuse within their homes than are severely injured in acts of violence on school grounds or elsewhere.

**Child victims are at greater risk of becoming offenders themselves.** Being abused or neglected as a child increases the likelihood of arrest as a juvenile by 53 percent and of arrest for a violent crime as an adult by 38 percent.

**Children suffer severe emotional and developmental consequences from exposure to violence.** Approximately 2 million adolescents ages 12–17 appear to have suffered from posttraumatic stress disorder (a long-term mental health condition characterized by a variety of behavioral and psychological symptoms), presumably stemming from violent experiences in their past.

## Addressing prevention, intervention, and accountability

Policymakers and practitioners need to find a way to organize the complex information about children's exposure to violence and the range of available strategies for action. One way is to think about a continuum of prevention, intervention, and accountability.

- **Prevention** means stopping children's exposure to violence before it happens. It means reaching at-risk families early; investing in a full range of early childhood care and respite services; teaching conflict resolution skills; challenging norms that allow men and boys to use power, control, and violence to dominate women and girls; ending domestic violence; keeping violent images out of the home; and providing community resources needed to prevent violence.

- **Intervention** means improving the current system of services for children or creating new approaches so that the service system is responsive to the complexity of children's lives and is rooted in and defined by communities.

- **Accountability** means holding perpetrators of violence—against children and against the children's mothers and caretakers—accountable for their actions. It means regarding crimes against children as among the most serious of all offenses. It means taking steps to reform the justice system and its procedures to ensure that children are not retraumatized by the legal process and that perpetrators are brought to justice.

## Working across disciplines

The continuum of prevention, intervention, and accountability demands thinking across disciplines and considering the ways in which each profession has an obligation to participate at every stage in the process. This approach can stimulate the professional and community collaboration that is crucial for addressing children's exposure to violence.

# Children Exposed to Violence: A Blueprint for Action

Participants in the National Summit defined a series of eight operating principles to address children's exposure to violence:

- ■ Principle 1: Work together.

- ■ Principle 2: Begin earlier.

- ■ Principle 3: Think developmentally.

- ■ Principle 4: Make mothers safe to keep children safe.

- ■ Principle 5: Enforce the law.

- ■ Principle 6: Make adequate resources available.

- ■ Principle 7: Work from a sound knowledge base.

- ■ Principle 8: Create a culture of nonviolence.

## Principle 1: Work together

No one program has the resources or the expertise to develop a truly comprehensive response to children and families experiencing violence. Experience shows that coordinated responses to children exposed to violence can accomplish the following: reduce the number of interviews and other agency procedures a child undergoes, minimize the number of individuals involved in a case, enhance the quality of evidence discovered, provide essential information to family and child protection services agencies, help build comprehensive safety plans for battered women and their children, prevent the system from holding battered women accountable for the actions of the abuser, and generally minimize the likelihood of conflicts and finger-pointing among agencies with different philosophies and mandates.

In addition to collaborative practices, there is an equally pressing need for collaborative leadership. Collaboration must also go beyond service agencies, community-based organizations, and individual professionals to include affected families, youth, and other community members.

Collaboration can range from taking steps to coordinate the activities of various disciplines to jointly constructing a new and mutual helping system. It can mean joint training, consultation, or actual joint practice. The Action Plan provides many examples of specific collaborative action steps that can be taken by child protective services professionals, domestic violence advocates, healthcare professionals, judges, law enforcement professionals, attorneys, legislators, policymakers, researchers, and school personnel. The Action Plan also highlights specific programs that exemplify collaborative action.

## Principle 2: Begin earlier

Recent research on children's brain development shows that what happens very early in a child's life forms the core of his or her later capacity for learning, socialization, and success. A common assumption has been that very young children's exposure to violence does not matter because they do not know what is going on and will not remember it. In fact, for even the youngest child, the feelings of terror, hopelessness, rage, and anxiety are very real, as is the failure to make positive and meaningful social connections. Children exposed to violence must accomplish crucial developmental tasks in a persistent state of fear. This new information goes hand in hand with the recent realization that very young children constitute a significant proportion of the children who are exposed to violence. Violence prevention efforts must start much earlier, and all training for professionals working in this field must include information about very young children.

Beginning earlier means reaching at-risk families even before the child is born, providing support in the home to help new parents become capable and nurturing caretakers, identifying families that are isolated from kinship or community supports and connecting them to the community, providing respite and crisis care services to help parents and caretakers in times of stress or crisis and to enhance the safety of battered women with young children, providing developmentally targeted support for teen parents, and emphasizing training to help professionals in all disciplines work effectively with very young children. The Action Plan highlights programs that focus on very young children.

## Principle 3: Think developmentally

In many ways, there has been a failure to take into account the changing needs of children exposed to violence at different stages in their lives or to recognize that it is possible to help an older child overcome the impact of violence that may have occurred years ago. Too often, a child's age or developmental level is disregarded. Perhaps worse, the procedures and settings are often geared to the needs of adults, not to children at all. This is not an effective strategy. Instead, expectations for children's ability to understand, communicate, and participate must change as children grow and develop. Whenever intervention is necessary, it must be developmentally appropriate for the child. Each formative stage presents unique opportunities and requires a different perspective and a different set of tools.

Bringing prevention, intervention, and accountability systems in line with the developmental needs of children can be accomplished through four principal strategies: providing training and consultation on child development for all professional disciplines, making the physical environments where services are provided child-friendly, changing agency procedures so they are consistent with children's needs and capacities, and partnering with schools.

The Action Plan highlights programs relevant to the principle of thinking developmentally, including several new violence and delinquency prevention and intervention projects that are using age as the basis for defining participants.

## Principle 4: Make mothers safe to keep children safe

Discussions at the National Summit on Children Exposed to Violence repeatedly returned to three related and persistent assumptions that must be challenged as efforts to address the problem of children exposed to violence move into the 21st century.

The first two assumptions are that maltreatment of children and violence against women are completely separate phenomena and that children who witness violence are not significantly affected by it. These assumptions are contradicted by two decades of research confirming that adults and children are often victimized in the same family and by research indicating that even when children do not suffer physical injury, the emotional consequences of viewing or hearing violent acts may be severe and long lasting.

The third assumption that must be challenged is that the nonabusive parent in a domestic violence situation (the mother in 95 percent of the cases) should be held accountable for the actions of the abuser. The practice of blaming women who are victims of domestic violence for batterers' violence against them and their children belies the fact that most battered women care deeply about their children's safety and work hard to protect them both from physical assaults by a batterer and from the harm of poverty and of isolation that may result from leaving or reporting a batterer. Women's efforts to protect their children should be recognized and supported.

To make safety and stability for battered women and their children a reality will require shifts in traditional practices and a willingness to confront some complicated and vexing policy questions. To resolve some of these dilemmas, the Action Plan identifies several specific steps that can be taken by child protective services professionals, domestic violence advocates, healthcare professionals, judges and court staff, law enforcement professionals, and school personnel. The Action Plan also highlights examples of programs and projects that address the needs of battered women and their children.

## Principle 5: Enforce the law

Prosecutors and other law enforcement officials agree that, all too often, abusive conduct that would typically result in a felony conviction if committed against an adult stranger is charged and treated less seriously when the victim is a child. Even when perpetrators of child abuse and domestic violence are convicted, judicial oversight and supervision of offenders are too often inadequate. The criminal justice system has a responsibility to make changes that will hold perpetrators of violence against women and children accountable for their actions through vigorous enforcement of the law. Holding perpetrators accountable will require changes to statutes, rules, policies, and procedures.

The U.S. Department of Justice has a number of specific recommendations for action. Recommendations for State legislative reforms pertain to prosecution of fatal child abuse cases, rules of evidence in child abuse and molestation cases, speedy trials for cases involving child victims or witnesses, privacy protections for child victims, the assumption that children will tell the truth, and special procedures for testimony by children. Recommendations for policy and procedural reforms pertain to child victim/witness specialists in police and prosecutors' offices, caseload limits for prosecutors, specialized training for law enforcement professionals, management of violent behavior of domestic violence offenders, multidisciplinary investigation teams, volunteer advocates for child victims, and vertical prosecution (i.e., assignment of a single magistrate and prosecutor for the life of a case) of cases involving children exposed to violence. The Action Plan also highlights a number of dependency court improvement initiatives that are under way around the country.

## Principle 6: Make adequate resources available

When it comes to preventing and reducing the impact of children's exposure to violence, needs always seem to exceed resources. Tragically, the systems that support children and families are too often the first to be cut when budgets are tight. Resources are desperately needed for both prevention and intervention. Funding is particularly critical to involve community partners, reduce caseloads and provide resources for child protection services and other direct service providers, support and evaluate the effectiveness of offender rehabilitation programs, serve battered women who are seeking to create safety for themselves and their children, and offer a full range of therapeutic treatments needed by children exposed to violence and training in practices that are sensitive to the developmental needs of children. Addressing the needs of children exposed to violence is initially expensive. Yet over the long term, these expenditures prove extremely cost effective.

Making sure that adequate resources are available to address children's exposure to violence means making better use of what is currently available (by improving coordination and encouraging volunteerism) and securing substantial and sustained financial investments—both public and private—in families, communities, and the systems that support and protect them. The Action Plan identifies several ways that community-based service agencies, governments, healthcare professionals, and universities can make creative use of what is already available and cites examples of how to secure additional resources.

## Principle 7: Work from a sound knowledge base

Despite a strong foundation, much more solid research and data on children's exposure to violence are needed. The lack of information makes it difficult to select the most effective interventions and get them funded. A number of subjects need particular attention, including basic research on child development and resiliency, short- and long-term evaluations of a range of interventions, the effectiveness of coordinated community response efforts, and research that focuses on protective factors unique to particular communities, the impact of cultural competence in working with families, and the issue of overrepresentation of particular minority groups in the justice system.

Wherever possible, efforts to prevent and reduce the impact of children's exposure to violence must be based on solid research and must also be documented and evaluated so that future efforts can be improved on the basis of experience. Participants in the National Summit on Children Exposed to Violence identified three critical components of an effective research strategy: seeking input from community members, practitioners, and victims and, where possible, conducting research in active collaboration with them; fostering international collaboration to gain and share knowledge worldwide; and broadly disseminating research findings, best and promising practices, and community directories of resources and practices.

## Principle 8: Create a culture of nonviolence

The greatest success will be achieved when specific actions are taken within a larger social environment that can help sustain them. A culture of nonviolence that supports children, women, and families is the vital context to ensure success in preventing and reducing the impact of children's exposure to violence. New studies are revealing two important facts: that the presence of "protective factors" (e.g., strong family relationships and alternative supports, among others) can guard children against the negative effects of exposure to violence and that "collective efficacy" (the willingness of neighbors to intervene on behalf of others) is the one characteristic that can account for less violence in a community. There is evidence to suggest, then, that a culture supportive of families, women, and children would inherently provide the protective factors and the collective efficacy needed to keep children safe from violence. Many believe in the value of such primary prevention, but specific skills and training are needed to develop effective primary prevention strategies and initiatives.

Cultural change is a tall order. The Action Plan outlines a number of critical steps that agencies, communities, and individuals can take to achieve this goal. Agencies can take steps to ensure meaningful citizen involvement, bring new voices to the table, and use the bully pulpit. Communities and individuals can focus on creating safe spaces, increasing awareness about children's exposure to violence, stopping gun violence, holding the media accountable, and supporting community policing. The Action Plan also cites examples of programs contributing to the creation of a nonviolent culture.

# Conclusion

Children's exposure to violence is an issue that touches everyone—an American tragedy that scars children and threatens the safety of communities. A great challenge lies ahead: to help move this country closer to the day when children are no longer victims of and witnesses to violence, when they are given the support they need to thrive, and when they respond to conflict nonviolently, without destroying their lives and the lives of others. Taking the steps in this national Action Plan will bring significant progress in this journey.

# Introduction

## Message From the Deputy Attorney General

Unfortunately, children are exposed to violence at nearly every turn. Violence is in the media, our communities and schools, and, most tragically, in children's homes.

Children suffer serious and long-term consequences from experiencing violence: children who are victims of, or witnesses to, violence are at an increased risk for development of behavioral, psychological, and physical problems. They are also more likely to engage in alcohol and drug use, delinquent acts, and later adult criminality. Furthermore, these children are often at risk of repeating the violence they have experienced, thus perpetuating a cycle of violence that can continue throughout future generations. We must stop this cycle of abuse now and take concrete action to prevent it from occurring in the future.

To address the impact of children's exposure to violence, 150 practitioners and policymakers from diverse disciplines came together in June 1999 to identify key issues that must be addressed to reduce and, ultimately, prevent children's exposure to violence. Participants at this meeting identified and committed to common goals and the following eight principles for action: work together, begin earlier, think developmentally, make mothers safe to keep children safe, enforce the law, make adequate resources available, work from a sound knowledge base, and create a culture of nonviolence.

This publication provides practical steps that can be implemented by professionals who serve youth and families, including child welfare and domestic violence advocates; healthcare practitioners; law enforcement, prosecutors, and judges; and legislators and policymakers. The document also provides general areas for action, identifies resources, and highlights programs that are currently making a difference in our children's lives.

I am certain that this Action Plan will assist you in your work on behalf of children, and your contribution and continued involvement in this effort are critical to its success. Through our partnerships at Federal, State, and local levels, we can make great progress in preventing and reducing children's exposure to violence, ensuring a better future for our Nation's communities, families, and youth.

**Eric H. Holder, Jr.**
*Deputy Attorney General*

# Setting the Stage: The Origins of "Safe From the Start"

## The stakes are high . . .

*I've never forgotten this child, because when I asked her to tell me about her picture, she said: "I'm screaming and no one hears me."*

—Eliana Gil, Ph.D.,
registered Art and Play Therapist

The likelihood that today's children will be exposed to some form of violence is enormous.

Every day, there are reports about violence in communities and families and about the children who are either the victims of or witnesses to it. Children encounter violence in the streets, at school, and in their own homes. They are bombarded by images of violence on television, in movies, and in video games. In short, the likelihood that today's children will be exposed to some form of violence is enormous. Tragically, too many children never experience a basic level of physical and emotional safety.

What happens to these children? In the short term, exposure to violence can result in the total upheaval of a child's life. First, there is the pain and suffering that comes from being abused or seeing a parent, another loved one, or a friend or an acquaintance hurt. Caregivers, parents, and professionals may disbelieve a child's account of violence experienced or witnessed, minimize the violence, or withdraw affection from the child. The child may be threatened with further harm or with harm to a loved one. If the report of abuse is not properly documented, nothing may be done about the abuse. Alternatively, a suspected abuser may be arrested, but then havoc may arise in the family, including loss of financial support and recriminations from family members. Children may be removed from the home and placed in foster care—separated from their family, friends, pets, and school.

What happens next? Children exposed to violence often experience heightened levels of depression and feelings of hopelessness, helplessness, anxiety, fear, rage, and aggression. They can have great difficulty making friends and sustaining relationships, accomplishing developmental tasks, and participating in everyday activities like school and play.

What awaits these children in the future? In many cases, they imitate what they have experienced: children exposed to violence are at greater risk of becoming offenders themselves. The Nation is facing the consequences of previous inadequate investments to protect its children. Childhood experiences affect a lifetime, and too many youth are reenacting the violence they have experienced, damaging their lives and the lives of others through criminal violence. There are also, of course, enormous consequences for those children

T here are many opportunities to intervene across the age span—it is never too early or too late.

who do not become violent offenders: many experience difficulties in school, at work, and in relationships; have physical and mental health problems; and may be at risk of being revictimized by violence throughout their lives. Thus, every day that society fails to address this tragedy increases the suffering of future generations.

## . . . But success is possible by taking action

Most children are remarkably resilient. This means that the way society understands and responds to the violence children experience can determine its impact on their lives in the long run. The term "children exposed to violence" can mean a number of things: experiencing physical or sexual abuse or neglect by a parent or caretaker, being assaulted by an acquaintance or stranger, or witnessing violence at home or at the home of a friend, at school, in the community, or through the media. The impact of these different kinds of violence varies greatly and depends on a number of factors, such as frequency, predictability, the age of the child, and the nature of the relationship between the perpetrator and the child. This variability, in turn, requires flexibility in the type and depth of interventions available.

There are many opportunities to intervene across the age span—it is never too early or too late. Prevention strategies can reduce the incidence of trauma. Providing early treatment that is appropriate to children's needs can help them begin to heal. Bringing perpetrators of violence to justice supports efforts to prevent and treat abuse and sends a clear message about the consequences of future violence. Professionals of all kinds have the power to respond effectively and sensitively and to work together. The means to meet this challenge exist, and the challenge must be met.

> *My dad was chasing my mom around the house with a knife. He was smiling. He hit my mom with a knife and he started frowning.*
>
> —5-year-old boy

## Safe From the Start: The National Summit on Children Exposed to Violence

> *These children are the reason we are here . . . not just to talk about the problems, and not just to preach to the choir, but to galvanize the knowledge and skills we have garnered over the decades in working with young people and families . . . if we want to see a movement catch fire, then it will be up to us to set it on fire with our passion and our commitment.*
>
> —Shay Bilchik, Former Administrator, U.S. Department of Justice, Office of Juvenile Justice and Delinquency Prevention; currently Executive Director, Child Welfare League of America

For 3 days in June 1999, the U.S. Departments of Justice and Health and Human Services (HHS), with the leadership of U.S. Deputy Attorney General Eric Holder, convened a summit of 150 practitioners and policymakers to build on their commitment to a common goal, think through the problem of children exposed to violence, and create a framework for a national blueprint for action.

Summit participants included many of the Nation's leaders in analyzing how to help children and in making solutions a reality. Professionals from both the public and private sectors joined together, representing child protective services; domestic violence services and advocacy; juvenile and family courts; law enforcement and prosecution; mental health, substance abuse, and healthcare services; family violence prevention services; childhood education and services; and State legislatures. Participants also included members of the National Advisory Council on Violence Against Women chaired by Attorney General Janet Reno and HHS Secretary Donna E. Shalala. With such a diverse group of professionals, the Summit was, in effect, a demonstration of one of its own key recommendations: collaboration across disciplines. Participants worked to find common ground across their different professional vocabularies, assumptions about the nature of the problem, and views on the solutions. In the end, the National Summit on Children Exposed to Violence, also known as the Safe From the Start Summit, provided the opportunity to learn from participants' experience and expertise and to craft a set of key operating principles and concrete steps: a practical action agenda—for local, State, and national leaders; professionals across disciplines; communities; and parents, youth, and families—to help prevent and reduce the impact of children's exposure to violence.

This Action Plan integrates the most up-to-date data on children exposed to violence with the key elements of known best practices. It suggests both discipline-specific and general action steps. It also identifies resources for additional information.

# A Framework for Understanding and Addressing Children's Exposure to Violence

> *I thought that it was my fault . . . that I was doing something*
> *wrong and that's why I would get in trouble if I talked about it.*
>
> —Young person exposed to violence

Efforts to address children's exposure to violence must incorporate a number of key elements. They must:

■ Reflect a commitment to common goals.

■ Be grounded in a full understanding of the issues and challenges involved.

■ Be based in fact.

The Summit was, in effect, a demonstration of one of its own key recommendations: collaboration across disciplines.

3

> **T**he goal must be a future in which children's lives and well-being are critically important to society and in which their safety is the highest priority.

- Fully integrate prevention, intervention, and accountability measures.
- Work across disciplines.

## Committing to common goals

As children move down the well-worn path from child victim to adult offender, there are many opportunities to stop the cycle of violence. The first step in meeting the challenge is commitment—commitment to a vision for the future and to a path for getting there. The goal must be a future in which children's lives and well-being are critically important to society and in which their safety is the highest priority—a future in which one can walk into any courthouse in this country and encounter no child who has been bruised, battered, or neglected; no child who has seen his or her mother[1] brutalized or demeaned; and no juvenile who has engaged in delinquent behavior.

Professionals and citizens must commit to doing things differently. If the ledger is not shifted so that more resources are spent on prevention, communities always will be cleaning up afterwards. If the justice system does not take the victimization of children seriously, how can it ask communities to do so? If professionals do not help battered women develop safety strategies and find necessary support services, how can they help the children of these women be safe and healthy? If children are not consistently viewed within the context of family, how can families be expected to succeed? How can those in need operate within and between systems that are not comprehensive and do not work together?

Finally, there must be a commitment from professionals to keep children and their voices at the core of this work. This means being able and willing to listen to their stories and use the information to help protect them. It means understanding the emotional impact of violence on children from the children themselves—not only as indicated clinically and statistically, but as demonstrated by children in their pictures and words.

> *One of the most important things that should come out of listening to children's voices is that it diminishes in all of us the impulse to deny the magnitude of what's going on.*
>
> —Pamela Sicher Cantor, M.D., Founder and President, Children's Mental Health Alliance Foundation

Only by looking through children's eyes and listening to their voices is it possible to begin to understand the destructive effects of violence on their lives. Only through understanding their experiences is it possible to begin to craft prevention, intervention, and accountability strategies that work.

# Understanding the challenges

In many ways, America is intently focused on violence. Recent high-profile incidents have led to debates over gun control, the role of the media, and the question of whom to hold accountable. Indeed, events such as the "Million Mom March" to stop gun violence show that Americans have vowed to renew their commitment to ending violence. Yet despite all the discussion and professed commitment, successfully identifying and implementing the solutions remain difficult. Why is this so?

■ **It is a complicated issue.** Children's exposure to violence (how and why it happens, what its consequences are, and what to do about it) is a complicated, multifaceted issue. A steady stream of new data and information about it only increases the complexity. As a result, standard operating definitions (e.g., "child abuse" or "domestic violence") often differ across professional, political, and geographical boundaries, and it can be difficult to agree upon joint strategies.

■ **It is a problem people try to avoid.** In many respects, the Nation shows a great reluctance to accept and do something about the fact that large numbers of children are harmed in lasting ways by violence. A number of dynamics are operative: (1) widespread denial about the traumatizing effects, (2) paralyzing discomfort with actually listening to children's stories, (3) refusal to believe that ostensibly upstanding citizens may be perpetrators, (4) social norms against "interfering" in the family life of others, and (5) emotional exhaustion ("burnout") among those who do get involved.

■ **It is an issue that divides professionals.** Too often, professionals working with children exposed to violence work in isolation from each other or, worse, at cross-purposes. The lack of coordination and collaboration is evident in persistent finger-pointing and blaming of one another for "dropping the ball." Yet professionals need to help each other make crucial decisions and ensure that their mutual efforts are in the best interests of the children and families they are serving.

These issues are among the many reasons why successfully responding to the problem of children exposed to violence has been so challenging—and why it is so critical to have a clearer understanding of the problem and some basic operating principles around which to organize the work. These issues are among the many that inspired the National Summit on Children Exposed to Violence.[2]

# Knowing the facts

Effective strategies for addressing children's exposure to violence must be based on a thorough understanding of the facts surrounding the problem. A review of the research on this topic reveals the scope and magnitude of the issue and suggests key entry points for intervention. The following sections highlight a few of these facts.

Children's exposure to violence is a complicated, multifaceted issue.

**C**hildren younger than age 4 accounted for 76 percent of child abuse and neglect fatalities in 1997.

## Millions of children are exposed to violence each year

■ National estimates based on a 1995 survey indicate that of 22.3 million children between the ages of 12 and 17, approximately 1.8 million have been the victims of a serious sexual assault, 3.9 million have been victims of a serious physical assault, and almost 9 million have witnessed serious violence.[3]

■ In 1997, young people (particularly teenagers) represented about 18 percent of arrests but made up about 25 percent of crime victims.[4]

■ Every day in 1997, six young people (under the age of 18) were murdered—56 percent of the victims were killed with a firearm.[5]

■ Estimates based on data from 44 States indicate that in 1997, approximately 984,000 children were victims of maltreatment nationwide and that approximately 1,100 children die annually as a result of child abuse or neglect.[6]

■ Data from 1992 indicate that before a child turns 18, he or she will have witnessed more than 200,000 acts of violence on television, including 16,000 murders.[7] It is highly likely that the numbers have increased since then.

■ Certain children are targeted as victims of crime more frequently, including those labeled "bad kids"; shy, lonely, and compliant children; preverbal and very young children; and emotionally disturbed or "needy" adolescents. Children with physical, emotional, or developmental disabilities are particularly vulnerable to victimization.[8]

## Young children are particularly at risk

■ A 1994 study found that 1 out of every 10 children treated in the Boston City Hospital primary care clinic had witnessed a shooting or stabbing before the age of 6. Almost all (94 percent) of the children had been exposed to multiple forms of violence, and half had been exposed to violence in the past month. Half of the children witnessed this violence in the home and half witnessed it on the streets. Their average age was 2.7 years.[9]

■ Domestic violence has been shown to occur disproportionately in homes with children under age 5.[10]

■ Children younger than age 4 accounted for 76 percent of child abuse and neglect fatalities in 1997. Child abuse is the leading cause of death in children under age 1.[11]

■ In one-third of all sexual assaults reported to law enforcement from 1991 to 1996, the victim was younger than age 12.[12]

■ Of the 2,100 juvenile murder victims in 1997, 33 percent were under age 6.[13]

## The maltreatment of children and violence against women often go hand in hand

- As many as half a million children may be encountered by police during domestic violence arrests each year.[14]

- Approximately 34 percent of rapes are estimated to occur in the victim's home, where children may be present to see or hear the sexual assault of their mothers or caretakers.[15]

- There is an overlap of 30 to 60 percent between violence against children and violence against women in the same families.[16]

- Children who are exposed to domestic violence are at increased risk of being murdered or physically injured.[17]

## The home can be a dangerous place

- Far more children are victims of serious physical abuse within their homes than are severely injured in acts of violence on school grounds or elsewhere.[18]

- Although sibling abuse is perhaps statistically the most common form of family violence, it is significantly underaddressed.[19]

## Child victims are at greater risk of becoming offenders themselves

- Being abused or neglected as a child increases the likelihood of arrest as a juvenile by 53 percent and of arrest for a violent crime as an adult by 38 percent.[20]

- On average, abused and neglected children begin committing crimes at younger ages. They also commit nearly twice as many offenses as non-abused children and are arrested more frequently.[21]

## Children suffer severe emotional and developmental consequences from exposure to violence

- The long-term consequences of childhood victimization can include mental health problems, educational difficulties, alcohol and drug abuse, and employment problems.[22]

- Approximately 2 million adolescents ages 12–17 appear to have suffered from posttraumatic stress disorder (PTSD)—presumably stemming from violent experiences in their past. PTSD is a long-term mental health condition characterized by depression, anxiety, flashbacks or nightmares, and other behavioral and psychological symptoms. A significant number of these adolescents abuse alcohol and drugs as a method of coping with PTSD.[23]

Being abused or neglected as a child increases the likelihood of arrest as a juvenile by 53 percent and of arrest for a violent crime as an adult by 38 percent.

Children who witness violence often experience many of the same symptoms and lasting effects as children who are direct victims of violence.

## Additional resources: Knowing the facts

**For more data on children exposed to violence, contact:**

Juvenile Justice Clearinghouse, P.O. Box 6000, Rockville, MD 20849; 800–638–8736; www.ojjdp.ncjrs.org/about/clearh.html.

National Center for Juvenile Justice (the research arm of the National Council of Juvenile and Family Court Judges), 710 Fifth Avenue, Suite 3000, Pittsburgh, PA 15219; 412–227–6950; www.ncjj.org.

National Center for Missing and Exploited Children, Charles B. Wang International Children's Building, 699 Prince Street, Alexandria, VA 22314; 800–843–5678 or 703–274–3900; www.missingkids.org.

National Center on Child Abuse Prevention Research (the research arm of Prevent Child Abuse America), 200 South Michigan Avenue, 17th Floor, Chicago, IL 60604; 312–663–3520; www.preventchildabuse.org/10ar97.html.

National Clearinghouse on Child Abuse and Neglect Information, 330 C Street SW., Washington, DC 20447; 800–FYI (394)–3366 or 703–385–7565; www.calib.com/nccanch.

National Resource Center for Safe Schools, Northeast Regional Educational Laboratory, 101 Southwest Main Street, Suite 500, Portland, OR 97204; 800–268–2275; www.nwrel.org/safe.

National Resource Center on Domestic Violence, 6400 Flank Drive, Suite 1300, Harrisburg, PA 17112; 800–537–2238.

Office for Victims of Crime Resource Center, P.O. Box 6000, Rockville, MD 20849; 800–627–6872; www.ojp.usdoj.gov/ovc/ovcres.

Resource Center on Domestic Violence: Child Protection and Custody, National Council of Juvenile and Family Court Judges, Family Violence Department, P.O. Box 8970, Reno, NV 89507; 800–527–3223; www.ncjfcj.unr.edu.

■ "Preliminary research indicates that, on average, children who experience domestic violence exhibit higher levels of childhood behavioral, social, and emotional problems than children who have not witnessed such violence."[24] They may experience feelings of terror, isolation, guilt, helplessness, and grief.[25]

■ The emotional consequences of viewing or hearing violent acts may be severe and long lasting. Children who witness violence often experience many of the same symptoms and lasting effects as children who are direct victims of violence.[26]

# Addressing prevention, intervention, and accountability

Committed to common goals, equipped with knowledge, and keeping the voices of children at the forefront, policymakers and practitioners need to find a way to organize the complex information and the range of available strategies for action. One way to do this it to think about a continuum of prevention, intervention, and accountability.

**Prevention** means, quite simply, stopping children's exposure to violence before it happens. It means reaching at-risk families early and helping new parents become capable and nurturing caretakers; investing in the full range of early childhood care and support efforts (including Head Start, Early Head Start, and childcare); providing outlets and respite for families under stress; teaching children, youth, and adults conflict resolution skills; challenging norms that allow men and boys to use power, control, and violence to dominate women and girls; bringing an end to domestic violence; keeping violent images out of homes; and ensuring that communities have the resources and capacity to support all of these efforts.

**Intervention** means improving the current system of services for children or creating new approaches so that the service system is responsive to the complexity of children's lives and is rooted in and defined by communities. Specifically, intervention must be seamless, flexible, collaborative across professional disciplines, oriented to the long term, and sensitive to cultural differences and children's developmental stages. Achieving these improvements to the service system will mean addressing issues of turf and prejudice, enhancing interdisciplinary communication, and improving training.

**Accountability** means holding perpetrators of violence—against children and against the children's mothers and caretakers—accountable for their actions. It means regarding crimes against children as among the most serious of all offenses. It means taking steps to reform criminal statutes, courtroom environments and procedures, and law enforcement and prosecutorial techniques to ensure that children are not retraumatized by the legal process and that perpetrators are brought to justice.

# Working across disciplines

Beyond providing an important set of goals and actions, the continuum of prevention, intervention, and accountability demands thinking across disciplines and considering the ways in which each profession has an obligation to participate at every stage in the process. Child protection workers, for example, have important roles not only in intervening once violence has occurred but in working with families to prevent further violence, in being available to the community to teach about prevention, and in collaborating with law enforcement to ensure that perpetrators are held accountable for their actions. Law enforcement

The continuum of prevention, intervention, and accountability demands thinking across disciplines and considering the ways in which each profession has an obligation to participate at every stage in the process.

**P**articipants in the National Summit arrived at a series of operating principles that can help organize and stimulate efforts to address children's exposure to violence.

personnel also have important roles to play in prevention and intervention. They should become educated about and sensitized to the dynamics of violence within families, with the goals of preventing violence before it occurs, identifying violence when it has occurred, and creating procedures for deposing and examining witnesses that encourage participation in the legal process without further trauma. The continuum of prevention, intervention, and accountability can stimulate professional and community collaboration that is crucial for addressing children's exposure to violence.[27]

## Where to begin? Eight principles for action

Participants in the National Summit arrived at a series of operating principles that can help organize and stimulate efforts to address children's exposure to violence. They are:

- Principle 1: Work together.

- Principle 2: Begin earlier.

- Principle 3: Think developmentally.

- Principle 4: Make mothers safe to keep children safe.

- Principle 5: Enforce the law.

- Principle 6: Make adequate resources available.

- Principle 7: Work from a sound knowledge base.

- Principle 8: Create a culture of nonviolence.

Each of these principles, detailed below, suggests a series of specific action steps.

## Children Exposed to Violence: A Blueprint for Action

*Healthy families and healthy communities go together. Violence prevention for children is not just an issue of law enforcement— it's much more. It's about creating safe places and learning opportunities, ensuring relationships with caring adults in the family and community, and providing a network of supports and services.*

—Ann Rosewater, Former Counselor to the Secretary of the
U.S. Department of Health and Human Services (HHS);
currently HHS Regional Director,
Atlanta, GA

# Principle 1: Work together

*Each profession has held a different piece of the puzzle making up a child's life, but no discipline could see the complete picture. As a result, children have fallen through the cracks.*

— Eric Holder, Deputy Attorney General of the United States

In some respects, the notion of "collaboration among diverse professionals" has come to feel like a flavor of the month. It sounds good and it makes sense, but too often what results is collaboration for its own sake. Yet when it comes to responding to the tragedy of violence, coordination among professionals is absolutely crucial. Children exposed to violence encounter a dizzying array of professionals (e.g., police, child protection workers, school counselors, domestic violence advocates, physicians, lawyers, therapists, judges), and whereas families must coordinate their interactions with these multiple practitioners, the agencies themselves are not required to coordinate their activities. Without coordination among this virtual crowd of helpers, children and their family members can be seriously retraumatized and may remain unprotected while perpetrators of violence go unpunished. Coordination is also critical to prevention. It creates a web of supports and protections that can provide a buffer against risks and can even eliminate (or at least postpone) the need for intervention.

In the final analysis, no one program has the resources or the expertise to develop a truly comprehensive response to children and families experiencing violence. Programs must work together. In fact, experience shows that coordinated responses to children exposed to violence can accomplish the following:

- Reduce the number of interviews and other agency procedures a child undergoes.

- Minimize the number of individuals involved in a case.

- Enhance the quality of evidence discovered.

- Provide essential information to family and child protection services agencies.

- Help build comprehensive safety plans for battered women and their children.

- Prevent the system from holding battered women accountable for the actions of the abuser (thereby increasing the danger to mothers and children).

- Generally minimize the likelihood of conflicts and finger-pointing among agencies with different philosophies and mandates.

*Collaboration is not having a meeting—the initial part is confrontation. You have to work out your differences before you can get to a common goal.*

—Pat McGrath, Deputy District Attorney, San Diego, CA

When it comes to responding to the tragedy of violence, coordination among professionals is absolutely crucial.

**C**ollaboration can range from taking steps to coordinate the activities of various disciplines to constructing a new and mutual helping system.

In addition to collaborative practice, there is an equally pressing need for collaborative leadership. Interdisciplinary leadership bodies—such as a State or community board, coordinating council, or task force—can monitor program availability, effectiveness, and inclusiveness; publicly articulate needs; and help secure resources for joint use. At the agency and intergovernmental level, collaborative leadership stimulates the development of supportive systems, offers frontline staff a vehicle for solving problems that may arise from collaboration, and raises the level of accountability for collective effectiveness.

Finally, collaboration must go beyond service agencies, community-based organizations, and individual professionals. It must include affected families, youth, and other community members while recognizing their differing levels of experience in, and readiness for, engaging in collaborative work. Too often, these voices are missing or are inadequately supported. As a result, agencies lose important information about how to design social support systems and services that are age-appropriate, culturally meaningful, and effective within local neighborhoods. Safety planning for battered women and their children is an excellent example of a multidisciplinary effort that actively involves the affected family members in the collaboration.

## Take action!

Collaboration can range from taking steps to coordinate the activities of various disciplines to constructing a new and mutual helping system. It can mean joint training, consultation, or actual joint practice. Many States have laws requiring joint investigations and cooperation between law enforcement and child protection agencies in child abuse cases. Other States have laws authorizing creation of multidisciplinary teams that bring together law enforcement professionals, child protective services professionals, domestic violence advocates and service providers, healthcare professionals, and other practitioners.

The following are examples of specific collaboration action steps that can be taken:

**Child protective services professionals.** Professionals providing child protective services can work with law enforcement professionals on integrated approaches to prosecution. For example, by seeking guidance from law enforcement about investigation and evidentiary issues, child protective services workers can enhance their contribution to prosecuting alleged perpetrators and keeping families and children safe.

Child protective services professionals also can work with domestic violence organizations to ensure that assessment and monitoring procedures will identify domestic violence, promote family safety, and support the child's relationship with the nonabusive parent. When domestic violence is an issue, they can work with staff from community-based organizations, battered women and other family members, and others who know the family to assess the child's immediate safety and determine what concrete steps can be taken to make the child safe.

**Domestic violence advocates.** Those who work as advocates in the area of domestic violence can support and organize regular cross-training activities with agencies and groups that work with families and children. Advocates can teach others why it is important to focus on the safety of mothers to ensure the safety of children. They can suggest strategies to build on the strengths of battered women and reinforce their safety. They also can work with child protective services and the courts to ensure that assessment procedures and advocacy efforts will identify child maltreatment and promote children's safety.

**Healthcare professionals.** In the healthcare field, professionals can use a team approach to intervening with child victims, taking advantage of the different skills of doctors, nurses (including school nurses), social workers, and other types of practitioners. Because of their leadership role in the healthcare field, doctors have a critical role to play in modeling how to work collaboratively with other healthcare professionals. Cooperation between healthcare professionals and child protection workers and domestic violence advocates should be proactive; i.e., it should take place before a joint intervention is necessary.

**Judges.** Judges can take a leadership role in knocking down the barriers between different courts (such as delinquency and dependency courts) and restructuring the system to facilitate sharing of information about families. For example, a judge should be aware that a 17-year-old perpetrator standing before him or her is also appearing in another court as a victim of abuse, that the youth's mother has been a victim of domestic violence and has a protection order on file, and that the youth's younger sibling has been picked up for truancy. At a minimum, judges need to collaboratively develop protocols for sharing information and issue orders that foster appropriate communication across agencies where possible.[28]

**Law enforcement professionals.** Law enforcement professionals can begin by acknowledging that because most officers are not child development specialists or mental health clinicians, it is critical to involve those who can provide expertise in these areas. Law enforcement professionals should have ready access to victim assistance professionals, advocates, and clinicians; involve them in the early stages to help manage cases; and ensure that support and services are provided to child victims and battered women on a continuing basis. In addition, training on child development—and on collaboration itself—can be incorporated into police academy training, ongoing officer training, and rollcall and can be arranged in conjunction with social workers or other professionals.

**Attorneys.** Attorneys can work through State and local bar associations to identify needed improvements in legislation, financing, and court operations. Some bar associations have created interdisciplinary task forces or commissions through which attorneys can work with a range of other professionals on this issue.

**Legislators and policymakers.** Elected officials can reassess confidentiality laws and practices that inhibit the sharing of information. In so doing, they need to remain sensitive to and protect the safety concerns of family members.[29]

E lected officials can reassess confidentiality laws and practices that inhibit the sharing of information.

**C** hildren's Advocacy Centers coordinate with social services agencies and mental and physical health providers to ensure that child victims and witnesses get the support they need.

**Researchers.** Evaluation is necessary at every step in the process—from the initial stages of planning collaborative efforts through joint data collection and the dissemination of findings. Researchers must be consistently and actively involved in collaborative efforts. (For more on the issue of research, see Principle 7.)

**School personnel.** All school personnel—teachers, counselors, administrators, school nurses, secretaries—should know their local child protective services workers so that when issues arise, they have ready access and established working relationships.

## Who's doing it?

**Children's Advocacy Centers.** In more than 350 communities around the country, Children's Advocacy Centers enable law enforcement officers, child protection workers, prosecutors, victim advocates, and therapists to coordinate the investigation, prosecution, and treatment of victims of child abuse and neglect. The Centers ensure cooperative interviews of children in a child-friendly setting, rather than multiple interviews in intimidating environments. Children's Advocacy Centers also coordinate with social services agencies and mental and physical health providers to ensure that child victims and witnesses get the support they need. The U.S. Department of Justice provides funds to communities seeking to establish or strengthen Children's Advocacy Centers.

*For more information,* write Nancy Chandler, Executive Director, National Children's Alliance, 1319 F Street NW., Suite 1001, Washington, DC 20004–1106; call 202–639–0597 (extension 101); e-mail info@nca-online.org; or visit www.nca-online.org.

**Community Based Family Resource and Support Program (CBFRSP).** The U.S. Department of Health and Human Services' Office on Child Abuse and Neglect administers CBFRSP, which is designed to fund collaborative, statewide child abuse prevention networks in each State. Within each State, the lead agency funds the direct provision of prevention services at the local level. One unique feature of this program is that it encourages States to use collaborative efforts to leverage additional funds that can then be matched by additional Federal dollars. Funds have typically been used to start up, maintain, and expand public information activities and provide parent information programs that focus on healthy and positive parenting skills and foster an understanding of child development and behavior.

*For more information,* write Ellie Wagoner, Federal Project Officer for Title II of the Child Abuse Prevention and Treatment Act, CBFRSP, Office on Child Abuse and Neglect Children's Bureau, U.S. Department of Health and Human Services, 330 C Street SW., Switzer Building, Room 2421, Washington, DC 22447; or call 202–205–0749. Local organizations may contact their State CBFRSP lead agency for information on funding and may also contact the National Clearinghouse on Child Abuse and Neglect Information (800–394–3366) or Ellie Wagoner for information about how to reach their State CBFRSP contact.

**The Child Development-Community Policing (CD–CP) Program.** This program is a joint effort of the Yale Child Study Center, the New Haven Police Department, local schools, and State child protective services. CD–CP is designed to provide immediate mental health services to child crime victims and witnesses. Mental health providers are available to respond with police officers at crime scenes where children are in need—24 hours a day. Police officers and child development/mental health specialists train each other. CD–CP also provides advocacy and therapeutic services for battered women and for their children who have witnessed violence in the home. Whether responding to a domestic violence call or an altercation in a schoolyard, police and psychologists work together to uncover the root causes of children's troubles and to help devise appropriate solutions.

*For more information,* write Colleen Vadala, Administrative Assistant, CD–CP Program, 47 College Street, Suite 212, New Haven, CT 06510; or call 203–932–2939.

**Palm Beach County's Community Partnership.** The Children's Mental Health Alliance and the Palm Beach County (Florida) Children's Behavioral Health Initiative are working together to place a behavioral health professional in each of the County's public schools. Beginning in elementary schools (with a focus on children in kindergarten through third grade), the project seeks to replace a system of fragmented and isolated programs with one that is coordinated and based on best practices for the delivery of children's mental health services. Behavioral health professionals work in the schools, collaborating with teachers to identify at-risk children. Once a child has been recognized, the behavioral health professional connects the family to available resources in the school and community. In addition to providing day-to-day support for the project in Palm Beach, the Children's Mental Health Alliance has a faculty of national and international experts to consult on best practices in behavioral health, model community partnerships, parent education models, and school-based antiviolence programs.

*For more information,* write Pamela Sicher Cantor, M.D., The Children's Mental Health Alliance, 52 East 72nd Street, New York, NY 10021; call 800–790–CMHA (2642) or 212–879–5244; or e-mail CMHAS@aol.com.

**Safe Kids/Safe Streets.** In this demonstration program supported by the U.S. Department of Justice, Office of Juvenile Justice and Delinquency Prevention (OJJDP), Executive Office for Weed and Seed, and Violence Against Women Office, five communities are working to break the link between child and adolescent victimization and later juvenile or adult criminality. The initiative seeks to reduce child and adolescent maltreatment and resulting child fatalities. Each Safe Kids/Safe Streets community is engaged in a full range of cross-agency strategies that are based on data and designed to improve the way the community responds to child abuse and neglect. Approaches include multidisciplinary investigation teams, case management and home visitation services, coordination between domestic violence and child abuse interventions, neighborhood-based family

I n the Safe Kids/Safe Streets program, five communities are working to break the link between child and adolescent victimization and later juvenile or adult criminality.

## Additional resources for Principle 1: Work together

**For more specific recommendations on collaborative practice, see the following publications:**

*Breaking the Cycle of Violence: Recommendations To Improve the Criminal Justice Response to Child Victims and Witnesses,* U.S. Department of Justice, Office of Justice Programs, Office for Victims of Crime, Monograph, June 1999, NCJ 176983 (for availability information, see p. x).

*Building Bridges Between Domestic Violence Organizations and Child Protective Services: A Policy and Practice Paper,* June 1999 (revised February 2000). Available from the National Resource Center on Domestic Violence (800–537–2238).

*Children Exposed to Violence: Recommendations for State Justice Systems,* U.S. Department of Justice, Office of the Deputy Attorney General, 1999, NCJ 180494 (for availability information, see p. x).

*A Coordinated Approach to Reducing Family Violence: Conference Highlights,* U.S. Department of Justice, Office of Justice Programs, National Institute of Justice and American Medical Association (AMA), Research Report, October 1995, NCJ 155184 (for availability information, see p. x).

*Effective Intervention in Domestic Violence and Child Maltreatment Cases: Guidelines for Policy and Practice,* recommendations from the National Council of Juvenile and Family Court Judges, 1999. To order, write National Council of Juvenile and Family Court Judges, P.O. Box 8970, Reno, NV 89507; or call 800–527–3223.

*Family Violence: Emerging Programs for Battered Mothers and Their Children,* National Council of Juvenile and Family Court Judges, 1998. To order, write National Council of Juvenile and Family Court Judges, P.O. Box 8970, Reno, NV 89507; or call 800–527–3223.

*Forming a Multidisciplinary Team To Investigate Child Abuse,* Portable Guides to Investigating Child Abuse, U.S. Department of Justice, Office of Justice Programs, Office of Juvenile Justice and Delinquency Prevention, November 1998, NCJ 170020 (for availability information, see p. x).

*Sharing Information: A Guide to the Family Educational Rights and Privacy Act and Participation in Juvenile Justice Programs,* U.S. Department of Justice, Office of Justice Programs, Office of Juvenile Justice and Delinquency Prevention, and U.S. Department of Education, Family Policy Compliance Office, June 1997, NCJ 163705 (for availability information, see p. x).

resource centers, community policing, dependency court reform, and prevention education.

*For more information,* including contact information for each of the Safe Kids sites, write Robin Delany-Shabazz, Coordinator of Child Abuse and Neglect Programs, U.S. Department of Justice, Office of Justice Programs, Office of Juvenile Justice and Delinquency Prevention, 800 K Street NW., Suite 300, Washington, DC 20531; or call 202–307–9963.

**Safe Start Initiative.** OJJDP is providing funding to expand community partnerships to prevent and reduce the impact of violence by creating a comprehensive service delivery system that will meet the needs of children and their families at any point of entry into the system. Partnerships between service providers—including the fields of childhood education and development, health and mental health, family support and strengthening, domestic violence and child welfare, substance abuse prevention and treatment, crisis intervention, courts and legal services, and law enforcement—should improve access to, and delivery and quality of, services for young children at high risk of exposure to violence and for those who have been exposed to violence. Safe Start is a multi-million dollar/5-year initiative.

*For more information,* write Kristen Kracke, Initiative Coordinator, U.S. Department of Justice, Office of Justice Programs, Office of Juvenile Justice and Delinquency Prevention, 800 K Street NW., Suite 300, Washington, DC 20531; or call 202–616–3649.

**The Violence Intervention Program (VIP) for Children and Families.** Based in New Orleans, LA, VIP is a partnership between the Department of Psychiatry at the Louisiana State University Health Sciences Center and the New Orleans Police Department. The program helps to identify and assist young children and families exposed to violence by providing education for police officers about the impact of violence on children, operating a 24-hour hotline, and developing a community resource directory to help police officers when they need to refer a child or family.

*For more information,* write Joy Osofsky, Founder and Director, Violence Intervention Program (VIP) for Children and Families, Louisiana State University Health Sciences Center, Department of Psychiatry, 1542 Tulane Avenue, New Orleans, LA 70112; call 504–568–3997; or e-mail josofs@lsumc.edu.

The Safe Start Initiative will meet the needs of children and their families at any point of entry into the system.

**N**ewly available information can help solve the puzzle of preventing and reducing the impact of children's exposure to violence.

## Principle 2: Begin earlier

*One of the greatest developmental challenges for toddlers is moving out and exploring the world. This beginning exploration requires courage and a certain degree of trust— that caretakers are there to protect and encourage them, and that the world they're moving into is basically safe. What happens when children get very early messages that this is not the case? Does it thwart their curiosity, their desire to learn, their ability to establish social relationships?*

—Betsy McAlister Groves, Director,
Boston Medical Center Child Witness to Violence Project

*Over half of the kids coming into the child welfare system are age 6 or below and historically we've done nothing to ask questions about them. We ignore these children as if we were blind to them. We must give each of these children a face.*

—The Honorable Cindy Lederman,
Presiding Judge of the Miami-Dade Juvenile Court

Newly available information can help solve the puzzle of preventing and reducing the impact of children's exposure to violence. For example, recent research on children's brain development shows that what happens very early in a child's life forms the core of his or her later capacity for learning, socialization, and success.

This information clearly indicates that efforts to date have not focused adequately on very young children and have been founded on the incorrect assumption that their exposure to violence does not matter because they do not know what is going on and will not remember it. In fact, feelings of terror, hopelessness, rage, and anxiety and a failure to make positive and meaningful social connections (responses commonly identified in older children exposed to violence) are very real for even the youngest child. For many children exposed to violence, the fear response is "turned on" all the time. Even in the presence of no external threat, these children experience the same feelings that other children who are not exposed to violence might experience in a state of high alarm. Children exposed to violence must accomplish crucial developmental tasks in this persistent state of fear.

*Experience early in life may be especially crucial in organizing the way the basic structures of the brain develop. For example, traumatic experiences at the beginning of life may have more profound effects on the "deeper" structures of the brain, which are responsible for basic regulatory capacities and enable the mind to respond later to stress.*

—Daniel Siegel, M.D., Medical Director,
Infant and Preschool Service, University of California,
Los Angeles; Associate Clinical Professor of Psychiatry,
UCLA School of Medicine; Director of Interdisciplinary Studies,
Children's Mental Health Alliance Foundation, New York[30]

This new information goes hand in hand with another relatively recent realization: that very young children constitute a significant proportion of the children who are exposed to violence. Domestic violence occurs disproportionately in homes with children younger than age 5;[31] children younger than age 4 account for 76 percent of child abuse and neglect fatalities;[32] and child abuse is the leading cause of death in children under age 1.[33] The ramifications are clear. Violence prevention efforts must start much earlier, and all training for professionals working in this field must include information about very young children.

## Take action!

Beginning earlier means:

- **Start before the child is born.** It is necessary to reach at-risk families even before a child is born. All medical providers, including public health departments and home visitation programs, should routinely assess for violence against women during pregnancy—it is perpetrated against up to 16 percent of pregnant women and may be a predictor of future child abuse.[34]

- **Start at home.** New parents need help and support to become capable and nurturing caretakers. The importance of bonding, attachment, and connectedness cannot be overstated.[35] Home visiting by trained professionals—especially nurses[36]—is a strategy that is demonstrating increasingly positive results. Expanding the availability of parenting education based outside the home also is important.

- **Reduce isolation.** Families that are isolated from kinship or community supports are at greater risk for violence. It is critical to figure out who these families are and connect them to the community. It is also necessary to develop specific strategies to counter batterers' deliberate isolation of their partners and families. Comprehensive support services and programs, including childcare, Head Start/Early Head Start, and recreational activities, are essential.

- **Prepare for emergencies.** Many of the children who are served by crisis nurseries and other respite programs witness violence every day. Respite and crisis care services can play a significant role in preventing violence by

Violence prevention efforts must start much earlier, and all training for professionals working in this field must include information about very young children.

U nfortunately, some youth who are victims of violence are themselves parents who may become perpetrators of violence against their own young children. Teen parents need developmentally based support.

providing parents or caretakers temporary relief or assistance in times of stress or crisis. In addition, domestic violence advocates are also key players in providing assistance, support, and shelter for women and their children in times of crisis.

■ **Remember youth.** Unfortunately, some youth who are victims of violence are themselves parents who may become perpetrators of violence against their own young children. Teen parents need developmentally based support.

■ **Train, train, train.** Professional training across disciplines should include information about the effects of violence on very young children, ways to work with these children and their families, and the dynamics of domestic violence.

## Who's doing it?

**Cradle to Classroom program.** A collaborative effort of the Chicago Public Schools, the Department of Public Health, six hospitals, and agencies for pregnant and parenting teens, this program trains teens in how to develop parenting skills and access community resources. It offers counseling to new mothers about issues of domestic violence and provides teens access to prenatal, nutritional, medical, social, and childcare services. The program has significantly reduced school drop-out and multiple birth rates among participating young women. By providing enhanced opportunities for parents to bond with their infants—increasing basic trust and security for the children—this program also lays the groundwork for skills and relationships later in life that may prevent violence.

*For more information,* write Sue Gamm, Chicago Board of Education, Specialized Services, 125 South Clark Street, Chicago, IL 60603; or call 773–553–2005.

**Crisis/respite care nurseries.** Respite—identified as one of the most important components of comprehensive family support—is a continuum of services ranging from planned, temporary childcare for children with disabilities or chronic illness to emergency care for children living in families facing a crisis such as job loss, serious illness, homelessness, or other serious stresses that can lead to child abuse. Crisis nurseries that provide this service have been demonstrated to protect against abuse and other negative consequences resulting from violence in the home. A survey of extremely high-risk families participating in the Lane County Relief Nursery Program in Eugene, OR, during the 1994–95 program year found that 95 percent of the several hundred enrolled children had no reports of abuse or neglect during their participation in the program, and 90 percent were living safely with their families at the end of the period covered by the survey. A 1992 study of Iowa crisis care programs indicated a 13-percent decrease in the reported incidence of child abuse in the initial four pilot counties after crisis care programs were implemented. Of the more than 25,000 children whose families used the services of the Vanessa Behan Crisis Nursery (a 24-hour, 7-day-a-week shelter program for at-risk children in Spokane, WA), not one has sustained a life-threatening injury since the nursery opened its doors in 1987.

*For more information,* write ARCH National Respite Network and Resource Center for Respite and Crisis Care, 800 Eastowne Drive, Suite 105, Chapel Hill, NC 27514; call 800–473–1727; or visit www.chtop.com.

**Healthy Families America (HFA).** This national initiative helps new parents get their children off to a healthy start. HFA provides home visiting services to families in more than 400 communities. Participation is strictly voluntary. The programs adhere to a series of critical elements: they must be intensive, comprehensive, long term, flexible, and culturally appropriate.

*For more information,* write Barbara Rawn, Director of Programs/HFA, Prevent Child Abuse America, 200 South Michigan Avenue, 17th Floor, Chicago, IL 60604; or call 312–663–3520.

**The Prenatal and Early Childhood Nurse Home Visitation Program.** Located in Denver, CO, the Nurse Home Visitation Program has been operating for more than 20 years. Nurses begin visiting low-income, first-time mothers during pregnancy and continue visits until a child is 2 years old. The program relies on trained, experienced, mature nurses with strong interpersonal skills. Nurses make home visits every 1–2 weeks and involve family members and friends. Each nurse carries a maximum caseload of 25 families. The program costs between $2,800 and $3,200 per family per year, and rigorous studies show that it reduces the risk of early antisocial behavior in children and reduces the incidence of maternal child abuse, substance abuse, and arrests. It also has recently been shown to reduce juvenile offending.[37]

*For more information,* write Peggy Hill, Associate Director, Kempe Prevention Research Center for Family and Child Health, 1825 Marion Street, Denver, CO 80218; or call 303–864–5207.

---

## Additional resources for Principle 2: Starting earlier

**For additional information on this topic, see:**

*Caring for Infants and Toddlers in Violent Environments: Hurt, Healing and Hope,* December 1993/January 1994; and *Islands of Safety: Assessing and Treating Young Victims of Violence,* April/May 1996; publications of Zero to Three, the National Center for Infants, Toddlers and Families. To order, call 800–899–4301 or visit www.zerotothree.org.

Starting Early Starting Smart: An Early Childhood Collaboration Between the U.S. Departments of Health and Human Services and Education and the Casey Family Program, www.samhsa.gov/grant/primarycare/0709top htm.

---

The Healthy Families America national initiative helps new parents get their children off to a healthy start

# Principle 3: Think developmentally

*Prevention is better than treatment, earlier is better than later, but it's never too late to make a difference.*

—Jack Shonkoff, M.D., Chairman,
National Academy of Sciences Board on
Children, Youth and Families

New information about very young children can help reshape thinking on how to prevent and treat their exposure to violence and how to hold perpetrators accountable for their actions. But violence happens not only to the very young—it happens to children of all ages. Yet, in many ways, there has been a failure to take into account the changing needs of children exposed to violence at different stages in their lives or to recognize that it is possible to help an older child overcome the impact of violence that may have occurred years ago. Too often, a child's developmental level or age is disregarded. Perhaps worse, the procedures and settings are often geared to the needs of adults, not to children at all.

This is not an effective strategy. Instead, expectations for children's ability to understand, communicate, and participate must change as children grow and develop. The capacity to engage with them at each stage of development requires specific skills and training. Outreach to children should shift from home to school and then to clubs and community programs. As children grow, the people likely to be most effective with them may shift from their parents or other family members to teachers, coaches, or other adult mentors and eventually to peers.

The bottom line is that whenever intervention is necessary, it must be developmentally appropriate for the child. Each formative stage presents unique opportunities and requires a different perspective and a different set of tools. A coordinated community response to children exposed to violence needs to identify known points of risk—when regular development can be derailed and when prevention and assistance are most needed—and respond with the best and most age-appropriate interventions.

## Take action!

*We ask a great deal of children who have been victims or witnesses to crime when we ask them to participate in the criminal justice system. It is a system designed for adults, not for children . . . and if children cannot participate effectively in the criminal justice system, it may be impossible to protect them from future victimization and to hold the offenders accountable for their actions.*

—From *Breaking the Cycle of Violence Recommendations
To Improve the Criminal Justice Response to Child Victims and Witnesses,*
U.S. Department of Justice, Office for Victims of Crime[38]

---

T oo often, a child's developmental level or age is disregarded.

Bringing prevention, intervention, and accountability systems in line with the developmental needs of children can be accomplished through four principal strategies:

- Providing training for all professional disciplines on child development (with particular attention to the early years) and ensuring access to child development experts when necessary.

- Making the physical environments where services are provided child-friendly.

- Changing agency procedures so they are consistent with children's needs and capacities.

- Partnering with schools.

**Training**. The U.S. Department of Justice recommends that all criminal justice professionals who come in contact with children be trained to identify those who are exposed to violence as victims or witnesses and be informed of the impact of victimization on children. Criminal justice professionals assigned to handle cases involving child victims and child witnesses should have indepth training in forensic interviewing, child development, identification of abuse-related injuries, the emotional and psychological impact of abuse, and legal issues related to child victims and witnesses.[39]

This recommendation should be applied to professionals of all disciplines who come into contact with children exposed to violence. For example, domestic violence organizations should train staff regularly to understand, recognize, and respond to maltreatment in children of varying ages.

**Creating child-friendly environments.** Police stations and courthouses should have victim-witness advocates available at all times to provide skilled support and assessment for children as they go through the justice system. Judges can arrange the courtroom so that safe and separate waiting areas are available to prevent the child from encountering the defendant or the defendant's family. At a minimum, social services, medical facilities, and domestic violence agencies should have child-sized furniture, toys and drawing material, and light-filled and cheerfully decorated interview rooms.

**Creating developmentally sensitive procedures.** Judges can prevent trauma to children in the court by, for example, making sure that all objections are argued outside the hearing or presence of the child, requiring that all attorneys use developmentally appropriate language when questioning child witnesses, and limiting continuances. In addition to modifying court procedures, courts should enforce rules of evidence to ensure that juries hear credible out-of-court statements that children make about abuse. Courts also should provide privacy protections for children and minimize the number of times a child is interviewed. Closed-circuit television or similar accommodations should be used as needed.

The U.S. Department of Justice recommends that all criminal justice professionals who come in contact with children be trained to identify those who are exposed to violence as victims or witnesses and be informed of the impact of victimization on children.

**S** chools are natural partners for implementing strategies to meet the developmental needs of children exposed to violence.

Systems should be put in place to coordinate social services interviews with mental and physical health examinations and with law enforcement investigations. The goal should be to minimize the number of interviews to which children are subjected.

Mental health services that are developmentally appropriate must be created for children. Child protective services also should be certain to screen for domestic violence and carefully assess the child's safety. Collaboration with domestic violence advocates, child development specialists, and others is essential for providing the best resources to children.

**Partnering with schools.** Schools—including Early Head Start, Head Start, and other preschool programs—are natural partners for implementing strategies to meet the developmental needs of children exposed to violence. Schools have extensive, age-specific experience and expertise with children. Schools also have mechanisms in place for providing preventive information to youth and families, flagging problems early, and intervening and working with families. For example, families are likely to find schools more familiar (and therefore less threatening) than social service or law enforcement agencies. Child protective services professionals, domestic violence advocates, healthcare professionals, law enforcement professionals, and other practitioners should take advantage of the resources provided by schools, actively engaging school personnel as consultants and partners.

## Who's doing it?

**Age-specific programs.** In a few places around the country, new violence and delinquency prevention and intervention programs for children are using age as the basis for defining participants.

■ In Boston, MA, the Child Witness to Violence Project (CWVP) provides counseling, advocacy, and outreach for children age 8 or younger who witness violence. The project has a multilingual, multicultural staff of social workers, early childhood specialists, and mental health professionals and is run under the auspices of the Department of Developmental and Behavioral Pediatrics at Boston Medical Center.

*For more information,* write Betsy McAlister Groves, Project Director, CWVP, Boston Medical Center, MAT 5, Boston, MA 02118; or call 617–414–4244.

■ In Hennepin County, MN, the Targeted Early Intervention Program is an intensive, long-term intervention for children whose delinquent behavior is first identified when they are younger than 10.

*For more information,* write Kristi Lahti-Johnson, Hennepin County Attorney's Office, Early Intervention and Protection Division, 525 Portland Avenue South, Minneapolis, MN 55415; or call 612–348–6223.

- In Los Angeles, CA, the LA Commission on Assaults Against Women developed the In Touch With Teens program to expose teenagers to the myths and realities of teen relationship violence and inform them about alternatives and resources for assistance.

  *For more information,* write Leah Aldridge, LA Commission on Assaults Against Women, 605 West Olympic Boulevard, Suite 400, Los Angeles, CA 90015; or call 213–955–9090.

- In Pittsburgh, PA, the Women's Center and Shelter of Greater Pittsburgh has created Violence Free: Healthy Choices for Kids, an elementary school prevention program that teaches fourth- and fifth-grade children alternative choices for handling interpersonal conflict, helps school personnel identify students living with domestic violence, and shows parents where and how to get help for partner abuse. The shelter provides the Healthy Choices program to 11 elementary schools in the Pittsburgh area.

  *For more information,* write Janet Scott, Women's Center and Shelter of Greater Pittsburgh, P.O. Box 9024, Pittsburgh, PA 15224; or call 412–687–8017 (extension 332).

- In Sacramento County, CA, the Community Intervention Program is geared to children ages 9 to 12 who are arrested or cited by law enforcement and whose families have been investigated at least once for child abuse and/or neglect.

  *For more information,* write Diane Telling-Rodriguez, Chief Deputy Probation Officer, County of Sacramento Probation Department, 3201 Florin-Perkins, Sacramento, CA 95826–3900; or call 916–875–0286.

- In Toronto, Canada, the Earlscourt Under 12 Outreach Project is a multifaceted intervention for boys between the ages of 6 and 11 who commit minor to serious offenses.

  *For more information,* write Leena K. Augimeri, Outreach Project, 46 St. Clair Gardens, Toronto, Ontario, M6E 3V4 Canada; call 416–654–8981 (extension 112); or visit www.earlscourt.on.ca.

**Child Victims Model Courts Project.** Since 1995, 18 courts around the country have used the support of this project to adopt model practices, including alternative dispute resolution; community-based services; multidisciplinary, court-led meetings and training; court calendar improvements; assignment of a single magistrate and prosecutor for the life of each case; more substantive preliminary hearings; and increased representation for children and families. The project is a joint effort of the National Council of Juvenile and Family Court Judges and the U.S. Department of Justice, Office of Juvenile Justice and Delinquency Prevention.

*For more information,* write the Permanency Planning for Children Department, National Council of Juvenile and Family Court Judges, P.O. Box 8970, Reno, NV 89507; call 800–527–3223; or e-mail ppp@pppncjfcj.org.

I n Pittsburgh, PA, Violence Free: Healthy Choices for Kids teaches fourth- and fifth-grade children alternative choices for handling interpersonal conflict.

## Additional resources for Principle 3: Think developmentally

**For more specific recommendations on developmentally appropriate practice or more information on research, best practices, and training opportunities, consult the following resources:**

American Academy of Pediatrics–Task Force on Adolescent Assault Victim Needs. Adolescent assault victim needs: A review of issues and a model protocol, *Pediatrics* 98(5):991–1001, 1996.

American Academy of Pediatrics–Task Force on Violence. The role of the pediatrician in youth violence prevention in clinical practice and at the community level, *Pediatrics* 103(1):173–181, 1999.

American Professional Society on the Abuse of Children (APSAC), 407 South Dearborn Street, Suite 1300, Chicago, IL 60605; 312–554–0166; www.apsac.org.

*Breaking the Cycle of Violence: Recommendations To Improve the Criminal Justice Response to Child Victims and Witnesses*, U.S. Department of Justice, Office of Justice Programs, Office for Victims of Crime, Monograph, June 1999, NCJ 176983 (for availability information, see p. x).

*Caring for Infants and Toddlers in Violent Environments: Hurt, Healing and Hope*, a publication of Zero to Three, the National Center for Infants, Toddlers and Families, December 1993/January 1994. To order, call 800–899–4301 or visit www.zerotothree.org.

*Children Exposed to Violence: Criminal Justice Resources*, U.S. Department of Justice, Office of Justice Programs, Office for Victims of Crime, Bulletin, June 1999, NCJ 176984 (for availability information, see p. x).

*Children Exposed to Violence: Recommendations for State Justice Systems*, U.S. Department of Justice, Office of the Deputy Attorney General, 1999, NCJ 180494 (for availability information, see p. x).

*Handbook on Questioning Children: A Linguistic Perspective*, by Dr. Anne Graffam Walker, American Bar Association, Center on Children and the Law, 1999. To order, call 800–285–2221.

*Interviewing Child Witnesses and Victims of Sexual Abuse*, Portable Guides to Investigating Child Abuse, U.S. Department of Justice, Office of Justice Programs, Office of Juvenile Justice and Delinquency Prevention, 1996, NCJ 161623 (for availability information, see p. x).

*Islands of Safety: Assessing and Treating Young Victims of Violence,* a publication of Zero to Three, the National Center for Infants, Toddlers and Families, April/May 1996. To order, call 800–899–4301 or visit www.zerotothree.org.

Missing and Exploited Children's Training Programs, Fox Valley Technical College Criminal Justice Department, P.O. Box 2277, Appleton, WI 54913–2277; 800–648–4966; www.foxvalley.tec.wi.us/ojjdp.

National Center for Prosecution of Child Abuse/American Prosecutors Research Institute, 99 Canal Center Plaza, Suite 510, Alexandria, VA 22314; 703–739–0321; www.ndaa-apri.org.

National Children's Alliance, 1319 F Street NW., Suite 1001, Washington, DC 20004; 800–239–9950 or 202–639–0597; www.nca-online.org.

National Clearinghouse on Child Abuse and Neglect Information, 330 C Street SW., Washington, DC 20447; 800–FYI(394)–3366 or 703–385–7565; www.calib.com/nccanch.

National Court Appointed Special Advocate (CASA) Association, 100 West Harrison Street, North Tower Suite 500, Seattle, WA 98119–4123; 800–628–3233 or 206–270–0072; www.nationalcasa.org.

National Resource Center on Child Maltreatment, Two Midtown Plaza, 1349 West Peachtree Street NE., Suite 900, Atlanta, GA 30309; 404–876–1934.

*Report to Congress: Youth Education and Domestic Violence Model Programs,* U.S. Department of Health and Human Services and U.S. Department of Education, 1998. To order, call William Riley, Director, Family Violence Prevention and Services Program, Administration for Children and Families, U.S. Department of Health and Human Services, at 202–401–5529.

Search Institute, 700 South Third Street, Suite 210, Minneapolis, MN 55415; 800–888–7828; visit www.search-institute.org.

Starting Early Starting Smart: An Early Childhood Collaboration Between the U.S. Departments of Health and Human Services and Education and the Casey Family Program, www.samhsa.gov/grant/primarycare/0709top.htm.

The School Resource Officers program combines the efforts of educators, law enforcement officers, students, and parents to prevent or deal with school-based violence.

**School Resource Officers program.** The Virginia Department of Criminal Justice Services sponsors training and grant funding for School Resource Officers (SRO's) throughout the Commonwealth. The SRO program combines the efforts of educators, law enforcement officers, students, and parents to prevent or deal with school-based violence. While SRO's are, first and foremost, law enforcement officers charged with keeping order, they also serve as law-related educators, role models, and community resources. The program is implemented differently in different jurisdictions, depending on local needs. For example, in Chesterfield County, a suburban community outside of Richmond, the police department places an SRO in each of the county's 11 middle schools and 9 high schools. In Bedford County, a large rural county in central Virginia, SRO's have collaborated with the Commonwealth's Attorney's Office and Juvenile and Domestic Relations Court to implement a "No Contact Contract" to address a bullying problem within the schools.

*For more information,* write Donna Bowman, Virginia Department of Criminal Justice Services, 805 East Broad Street, Richmond, VA 23219; call 804–371–6506; or e-mail dbowman@dcjs.state.va.us.

**King County Kids Court.** In this 5-hour, Saturday court school in Seattle, WA, child victims of crime meet with a judge and a prosecutor and participate in activities that help them understand the roles of court personnel, discuss their concerns about testifying in court, ask questions, and feel comfortable in the courtroom. Children and their parents also learn stress reduction techniques to help them through the trial. Kids Court has developed a comprehensive curriculum that is being replicated in several cities across the country.

*For more information,* write Donna Belin, Executive Director, King County Kids Court, Office of the Prosecuting Attorney, 704 228th Avenue NE., PMB 323, Sammanish, WA 98053; or call 206–386–KIDS(5437).

## Principle 4: Make mothers safe to keep children safe

> *I'm here because I think that if someone would have listened to what my mom was saying, she still could have been alive today. It's like nobody cared. Police were called to my house constantly and nothing was done. I just want you to listen to what I have to say because, I may only be 15, but I'm here because my mom couldn't be. And I'll do what I can for domestic violence no matter what it takes.*
>
> —Wendy H., youth participant in the
> National Summit on Children Exposed to Violence

As efforts to address the problem of children exposed to violence move into the next century, so too must some basic operating assumptions change with the times. While this broad dictum certainly could apply to many issues, discussions among participants in the National Summit on Children Exposed to Violence repeatedly returned to three related assumptions that still serve as the basis for much policy and practice. These assumptions must be challenged so that the groundwork can be laid for solutions that will be more successful than past efforts.

The first assumption is that maltreatment of children and violence against women are completely separate phenomena. The second is that children who witness violence are not significantly affected by it. The third is that the nonabusive parent in a domestic violence situation (the mother in 95 percent of the cases) should be held accountable for the actions of the abuser.

> *Family violence is rarely just a one-time event. When children witness abuse between their parents, there are no safe spaces. Violence committed by a loved one kills trust—and can have an enduring effect on how children learn to form relationships. . . . If we are to achieve our goals we must enable a child to heal and be safe, and to enable that child's mother—too often a victim of abuse herself—to achieve safety and stability. And we must seriously hold perpetrators accountable without further jeopardizing children and women's safety and the stability of that family.*

> —Ann Rosewater, Former Counselor to the Secretary of the
> U.S. Department of Health and Human Services (HHS);
> currently HHS Regional Director,
> Atlanta, GA

**Child maltreatment and violence against women often happen under the same roof.** Although it would be difficult to discern from current policy and practice, two decades of research have confirmed that adults and children often are victimized in the same family. Data show that police encounter at least half a million children during domestic violence arrests each year;[40] there is an overlap of 30 to 60 percent between violence against children and violence against women in the same families; battered women are more likely to abuse their children than women who have not been battered;[41] and children who are exposed to domestic violence are at increased risk of being murdered or physically injured.[42]

Once the significant co-occurrence of child maltreatment and domestic violence is acknowledged, it will be possible to begin sensitive and successful interventions and improve the capacity to hold perpetrators accountable. The overlap of child maltreatment and domestic violence is one reason why collaboration between law enforcement, child protective services, and domestic violence programs is so critical.

Once the significant co-occurrence of child maltreatment and domestic violence is acknowledged, it will be possible to begin sensitive and successful interventions and improve the capacity to hold perpetrators accountable.

**R**esearch shows that even when children do not suffer physical injury, the emotional consequences of viewing or hearing violent acts can be severe and long lasting.

**Violence exceeds the bounds of physical harm.** Children witness violence—homicide, rape, assault, and domestic violence—every day. Research shows that even when children do not suffer physical injury, the emotional consequences of viewing or hearing violent acts can be severe and long lasting. However, the issue is complex. The National Council of Juvenile and Family Court Judges reports:

> A wide range of studies has shown that some children who witness adult domestic violence suffer considerably. These studies indicate that, on average, children who experience domestic violence exhibit higher levels of childhood behavior, social, and emotional problems than children who have not witnessed such violence. These documented harmful effects to child development have led many to conclude that if a child resides in a home where domestic violence is occurring, the child is in immediate danger and requires child protection services.

> Research in this area is still in its infancy, however, and a large percentage of child witnesses in these studies did not show elevated levels of developmental problems. The impact of witnessing violence on children is moderated by a number of factors, with some children showing great resilience in the face of adversity. Each child's response to domestic violence, therefore, should be assessed carefully, and harm established clearly, before agencies and courts determine which interventions are required.[43]

**Battered (nonoffending) mothers are allies for those who are trying to protect the children.** Historically, women who are victims of domestic violence often have been held responsible for batterers' violence against them and their children. They have been blamed for being abused, for exposing their children to abuse, for not leaving the perpetrator, or for not stopping his violence. This blame belies the fact that most battered women care deeply about their children's safety and work hard to protect them both from physical assaults by a batterer and from the harm of poverty and of isolation that may result from leaving or reporting a batterer. They know that creating safety for children requires eliminating both of these sets of risks.[44]

> *We must listen to these mothers and recognize their heroism.*
> *The more we know about them and their lives, the better*
> *we are at communicating their strengths, which has*
> *resulted in needed policy changes.*
>
> —The Honorable Cindy Lederman,
> Presiding Judge of the Miami-Dade Juvenile Court

A battered woman cannot change or stop a perpetrator's violence by herself; if she does not have adequate support, resources, and protection, leaving him may simply make it worse for her children. In many cases, making mothers safe—by trying to remove or change the source of the domestic violence risk (i.e., the batterer)—does make children safer and offers them their best hope for stability. Therefore, child welfare administrators and juvenile court personnel should seek to keep children affected by maltreatment and domestic violence in the care of their nonoffending parent whenever possible.[45] Women's efforts to protect their children should be recognized and supported.

> *I never considered talking to the mother about what she wanted. I 'slayed the dragon,' but the dragon paid the rent and took care of the kids while mom was at work. . . . It's unfair to ask women and children to stick their necks out and risk their lives to help us prosecute cases when we are unwilling to look at what they really need.*
>
> —Pat McGrath, Deputy District Attorney, San Diego, CA

*W*omen's efforts to protect their children should be recognized and supported.

## Take action!

To make this vision of safety and stability for battered women and their children real will require shifts in traditional practices and a willingness to confront some complicated and vexing policy questions. For example, how can juvenile courts and others protect children of battered mothers without revictimizing and blaming the nonabusive mother? What should be done when a battered woman wants to protect her child but is unable to do so? What should child protection workers do when a batterer is back in the house and children are not safe? What can be done to support battered women so they are not forced to return to abusive relationships? Can battered mothers who abuse their children be supported and protected from harm and also be held responsible for child maltreatment and for changes in their behavior?[46]

The following are examples of specific action steps that can begin to resolve some of these dilemmas:

**Child protective services professionals.** Professionals in child protective services should take seriously the impact that witnessing violence has on children but should not automatically assume that allowing a child to witness violence constitutes maltreatment and requires removing the child from the home. Agency policy should clearly state the criteria under which children can remain safely with a nonabusing parent, the assessment required to determine safety, and the safety planning, services, support, and monitoring that will be required in these cases. Because of the variation in children's responses to exposure to domestic violence, decisions should be made on a case-by-case basis.

**Domestic violence advocates.** Advocates should keep the situation of children and families in mind as they work with victims. They should understand, recognize, and respond to child maltreatment and work collaboratively with child protection, law enforcement, and the judiciary to create safety and stability for families. Advocates should also develop greater capacity for serving mothers

L aw enforcement agencies should work for the safety of battered mothers and their children by holding the batterer—not the adult victim—accountable for domestic abuse.

from diverse backgrounds and those with multiple problems (e.g., mental health or substance abuse issues). They also should be aware of State laws requiring them to report suspected child abuse to the appropriate authorities.

**Healthcare professionals.** Staff in hospital emergency rooms, rape crisis centers, and outpatient pediatric and mental health clinics, for example, should know how to safely and accurately assess for the presence of domestic violence when they see victims of child abuse and for the presence of child abuse when they see victims of domestic violence.

**Judges and court staff.** Judges in domestic violence and child protection cases should give complete instructions that fully protect both the mother and her children. The instructions should provide for helping the victim develop a safety plan, should explicitly address the issue of weapons possession by perpetrators, and should include very carefully crafted custody and visitation orders. Judges should hold perpetrators in contempt if they violate conditions of the order and should follow up with the victims regarding how best to enforce the order. Judges also can be leaders in helping child protection and domestic violence services change the way they interact with one another. The Open Society Institute's Center on Crime, Communities & Culture recommends:

> The juvenile court should insist that a petition alleging 'failure to protect' on the part of the battered mother also alleges efforts she made to protect the children, the ways in which she failed to protect, and the reasons why, as well as identifying any perpetrator who may have prevented or impeded her from carrying out her parental duties. The juvenile court should prioritize removing any abuser before removing a child from a battered mother, and it should work with child welfare and social service agencies to ensure that separate service plans for the perpetrator and the victim of domestic violence are developed.[47]

**Law enforcement professionals.** Law enforcement agencies should work for the safety of battered mothers and their children by holding the batterer—not the adult victim—accountable for domestic abuse. Law enforcement agencies should make arrests, enforce protection orders removing the batterer from the home, and monitor batterer compliance with required services and counseling plans. In addition, every time police are called to a domestic violence incident, they should be aware that if children are present, it is important to assess whether they, too, have been abused. Policies and protocols should be in place for responding to such situations. Agencies should develop these policies and protocols in collaboration with domestic violence programs, child welfare agencies, mental health agencies, juvenile courts, the criminal justice system, and the community. Police on the scene also need to be aware of State law requirements for reporting child abuse and neglect. Agencies should consider creating a special unit with expertise in this area.

**School personnel.** In addition to watching for signs of exposure to violence among students, school personnel should be aware of the signs of domestic violence—and the probability of co-occurrence with child maltreatment—and be trained in how to respond effectively.

## Who's doing it?

**Casa Myrna Vazquez (CMV).** This bilingual and multicultural organization in Boston, MA, provides shelter and services to battered women and their children. CMV has two unique programs for teenagers. The Adolescent Transitional Living Program provides a supervised residence for up to 3 years for eight homeless, battered teenage girls who are pregnant or have infants. The young women receive comprehensive services and advocacy workshops in health, parenting, and housing. CMV also has a Moms and Sons Program to provide much-needed housing to battered women with adolescent male children. The program shelters 12 to 16 individuals or 4 families for up to 18 months and provides culturally appropriate clinical intervention and treatment, including intergenerational activities, recreation therapy, and mentoring from positive male role models.

*For more information,* write Casa Myrna Vazquez, Inc., P.O. Box 180019, Boston, MA 02118; or call 800–992–2600 or 617–521–0100.

**Dade County Dependency Court Intervention Program (DCIP) for Family Violence.** To date, the Dade County (Florida) DCIP may be the Nation's only court program designed to address the co-occurrence of child maltreatment and other forms of family violence, to deal with domestic violence in the context of the child protection system, and to bring battered women's advocacy to child dependency proceedings. DCIP seeks to raise awareness in the child welfare system that children are at increased risk for additional harm when domestic violence and child maltreatment co-occur. It also seeks to provide outreach-based advocacy for battered mothers, learn more about the impact of domestic violence, provide advocacy and service for battered mothers, and lead the development of a coordinated community response. DCIP operates on the assumption that the most effective way to make a child safe is to enhance the safety of the mother.

*For more information,* write The Honorable Cindy Lederman, Dependency Court Intervention Program, 3300 NW. 27th Avenue, Room 201, Miami, FL 33142; or call 305–638–6087.

**DOJ/HHS demonstration project.** In the fall of 2000, the U.S. Departments of Justice and Health and Human Services will begin implementing a demonstration initiative in selected communities that are interested in better addressing the intersection of domestic violence and child maltreatment. Five communities will conduct demonstration projects based on the guidelines established by the National Council of Juvenile and Family Court Judges in *Effective Intervention in Domestic Violence and Child Maltreatment Cases: Guidelines for Policy and Practice.* The initiative will seek to facilitate more effective interventions for battered women and their children involved with three systems: child welfare

The Dade County (Florida) Dependency Court Intervention Program operates on the assumption that the most effective way to make a child safe is to enhance the safety of the mother.

> **D**omestic violence specialists consult with child protection workers throughout the Commonwealth and provide case consultation, direct advocacy, and linkages to community resources.

agencies, domestic violence service providers, and dependency courts. Strategies may include increasing collaboration between systems, developing and implementing cross-system policy and staff development, improving procedures within each system, holding batterers accountable, and seeking greater community resources for serving affected families. A national evaluator will assess whether the initiative promotes more effective collaboration between local partners than previously and whether the initiative helps women and children achieve greater safety.

*For more information,* write Jerry Silverman, U.S. Department of Health and Human Services, Office of the Assistant Secretary for Planning and Evaluation, 200 Independence Avenue SW., Room 450G, Washington, DC 20201; call 202–690–5654; or e-mail jsilverm@osaspe.dhhs.gov.

**Massachusetts Department of Social Services Domestic Violence Unit.** Ten years ago, the Commonwealth of Massachusetts began to build a Domestic Violence Unit within its child protective services program. This was the Nation's first systemwide effort to bring domestic violence expertise to bear on decisionmaking within child protective services. Domestic violence specialists consult with child protection workers throughout the Commonwealth and provide case consultation, direct advocacy, and linkages to community resources. As a result of the program, Massachusetts protective services workers identified domestic violence as an issue to be addressed in 48 percent of their cases in 1994.

*For more information,* write Pam Whitney, Director, Massachusetts Department of Social Services Domestic Violence Unit, 24 Farnsworth, Boston, MA 02210; or call 617–748–2338.

**Oregon's State Office for Services to Children and Families (SCF).** Oregon's State child protection services and welfare agency, SCF, is working in collaboration with the Oregon Coalition Against Domestic Violence to develop and evaluate specialized services for victims of domestic violence who are referred to child protective services. The project's goals are to increase the safety of battered women and their children referred to child protective services and to decrease the practice of blaming victims. Its strategies are to enhance collaboration between local SCF branches and domestic violence programs and to develop and evaluate specialized, effective services for battered women served by SCF. The agency is contracting with three local domestic violence programs to place advocates in rural jurisdictions. Housed at the local SCF offices, advocates provide consultation to SCF workers and direct services to clients. Services include assessment of domestic violence, creation of safety plans, advocacy, and peer support.

*For more information,* write Bonnie Braeutigam, Domestic Violence Program Coordinator, State Office for Services to Children and Families, Child Protection Unit, 500 Summer Street NE., E–68, Salem, OR, 97310–1067; or call 503–945–6686.

## Principle 5: Enforce the law

> *It is a sad reality that the criminal justice system often does not deal adequately, and in my mind justly, with crimes against children. . . . It is time, way past time, for us to look at children's exposure to violence as a law enforcement issue as well as a social services issue.*
>
> —Eric Holder, Deputy Attorney General of the United States

> *A crime against a child is a crime. The suggestion that these cases should be handled in mediation—instead of in the justice system—is wrong. If the justice system can't handle it, the system needs to change.*
>
> —J. Tom Morgan, District Attorney, Decatur, GA

P rosecutors and other law enforcement officials agree that, all too often, abusive conduct that would typically result in a felony conviction if committed against an adult stranger is charged and treated less seriously when the victim is a child.

Prosecutors and other law enforcement officials agree that, all too often, abusive conduct (sexual, physical, sometimes even homicidal acts) that would typically result in a felony conviction if committed against an adult stranger is charged and treated less seriously when the victim is a child. They see too many cases in which a child has died as the result of repeated physical abuse by an alleged "caretaker" and the defendant successfully argues that he or she never intended to hurt the child or never intended for the child to die. In the not-so-distant past,

**T**he criminal justice system has a responsibility to make changes that will hold perpetrators of violence against women and children accountable for their actions through vigorous enforcement of the law.

in fact, the death of a child as a result of chronic child abuse or severe neglect was not recognized under most State laws as an intentional homicide and often was not prosecuted to the fullest extent. The tragic result is that perpetrators of violence against children may be free to commit their crimes again. Domestic violence victims have suffered from a similar lack of response and advocacy from the legal system.

Tougher sentencing, however, may not be enough. Even when perpetrators of child abuse and domestic violence are convicted, judicial oversight and supervision of offenders are too often inadequate. Aggressive followup is critical to protecting children and their mothers.

> *We judges don't follow up on our orders. We have to bring batterers in, and create a legal and judicial culture of safety that prevents future harm.*
>
> —The Honorable Ernestine Gray, Administrative Judge, Orleans Parish (Louisiana) Juvenile Court

Why are the laws not fully upheld? Probable reasons include cultural prohibitions against intervening in "family matters," this Nation's early history of treating women and children as property and not according them basic rights, and continued bias and discrimination against women. Regardless of the origins of the problem, the criminal justice system has a responsibility to make changes that will hold perpetrators of violence against women and children accountable for their actions through vigorous enforcement of the law.

The court and law enforcement improvement strategies detailed under Principle 3 of the Action Plan are designed to protect children from retraumatization by the criminal justice system (and other systems). As noted, an important byproduct of these changes is a greater likelihood of successful prosecution. Yet ensuring accountability goes beyond helping children be more effective witnesses in court. Holding perpetrators accountable will also require changes to statutes, rules, policies, and procedures.

> *You should never be in a position where you can't hold a defendant accountable because you don't want to put a 5-year-old through the trauma. We have to change the rules.*
>
> —Pat McGrath, Deputy District Attorney, San Diego, CA

## Take action!

A unified, statewide family court may be the ideal way to address many of these issues, but in the absence of such a system, much can be accomplished through legal and procedural changes. The U.S. Department of Justice has a number of specific recommendations for action that will help hold perpetrators of violence against children accountable for their actions. These are listed below.

**Enact State legislation to:**

- Reform murder statutes to allow prosecutions of fatal child abuse under "felony murder" provisions and to create special provisions addressing murders of children as part of a pattern or practice of child abuse.

- Adopt evidence rules to ensure that juries in child molestation cases can hear evidence that the defendant has committed similar crimes.

- Adopt evidence rules to ensure that juries hear credible out-of-court statements that children make about abuse.

- Speed up trials where children are the victims and/or witnesses.

- Provide privacy protections to children who are the victims of crime.

- Start with the presumption that children will tell the truth.

- Allow special procedures for child testimony on the rare occasions when a child cannot testify in the usual manner.

- Change the Federal rules of evidence so they are consistent with those in some of the more progressive States. Although the Federal rules do not technically affect local rules, legal arguments always refer to Federal rules as the basis for decisionmaking.

For more detailed information and sample legislative language on each of these and other recommendations, see *Children Exposed to Violence: Recommendations for State Justice Systems*, U.S. Department of Justice, Office of the Deputy Attorney General, 1999, NCJ 180494 (for availability information, see p. x).

**Change policies and procedures to:**

- Designate specialists or create special units in police departments and prosecutors' offices to handle child victims and witnesses (and/or make use of child interview specialists from another discipline).

- Maintain reasonable caseloads. A national survey of prosecutors found that of all cases, child abuse and adult sexual assault require the most time and resources.

- Provide training to prosecutors, judges, and police officers in forensic interviewing, child development, identification of abuse-related injuries, the emotional and psychological impact of abuse, and legal issues related to child victims and witnesses.

- Manage the violent behavior of domestic violence offenders through proactive and frequent judicial monitoring and the use of graduated sanctions (such as re-education programs for men who batter, community service, intense supervision, incarceration, and, when appropriate, testing and treatment for alcohol or substance abuse). In addition, judges should be open to input from diverse community-based organizations to jointly craft community-sensitive (and thus more effective) sanctions for domestic violence offenders. Probation and parole agencies, in collaboration with law

Manage the violent behavior of domestic violence offenders through proactive and frequent judicial monitoring and the use of graduated sanctions.

# Additional resources for Principle 5: Enforce the law

**For more specific recommendations for changes to criminal justice policies and practices, see:**

*Breaking the Cycle of Violence: Recommendations To Improve the Criminal Justice Response to Child Victims and Witnesses*, U.S. Department of Justice, Office of Justice Programs, Office for Victims of Crime, Monograph, June 1999, NCJ 176983 (for availability information, see p. x).

*Law Enforcement Response to Child Abuse*, U.S. Department of Justice, Office of Justice Programs, Office of Juvenile Justice and Delinquency Prevention, Portable Guides to Investigating Child Abuse, May 1997, NCJ 162425 (for availability information, see p. x).

*New Directions from the Field: Victims' Rights and Services for the 21st Century, Child Victims*, U.S. Department of Justice, Office of Justice Programs, Office for Victims of Crime, Bulletin, 1998, NCJ 172827 (for availability information, see p. x).

*Overview of the Portable Guides to Investigating Child Abuse: Update 2000*, U.S. Department of Justice, Office of Justice Programs, Office of Juvenile Justice and Delinquency Prevention, Bulletin (presents information about the guides in the Portable Guides to Investigating Child Abuse series), February 2000, NCJ 178893 (for availability information, see p. x).

*Sexual Assault Nurse Examiner (SANE) Development and Operation Guide*, U.S. Department of Justice, Office of Justice Programs, Office for Victims of Crime and Sexual Assault Resource Service, Minneapolis, MN, NCJ 170609 (for availability information, see p. x).

enforcement, should develop strategies for monitoring offenders and strictly ensuring that they meet the terms and conditions of probation and parole.

■ Create multidisciplinary investigation teams. (For more information about this strategy, see Principle 1.)

■ Establish a volunteer program for court-appointed special advocates and standardize training for volunteer advocates. These programs have traditionally been found in family or juvenile courts, but there has been an increase in the use of independent legal advocacy for child victims in criminal court proceedings.

■ Ensure vertical prosecution (assignment of a single magistrate and prosecutor for the life of a case) in cases involving children exposed to violence.

> **For an annotated directory of criminal justice resources on this issue, see:**
>
> *Children Exposed to Violence: Criminal Justice Resources,* U.S. Department of Justice, Office of Justice Programs, Office for Victims of Crime, Bulletin, June 1999, NCJ 176984 (for availability information, see p. x).
>
> **For information on research, best practices, and training opportunities, contact:**
>
> American Bar Association Center on Children and the Law, 740 15th Street NW., Washington, DC 20005; 202–662–1720; www.abanet.org/child/home.html.
>
> American Professional Society on the Abuse of Children (APSAC), 407 South Dearborn Street, Suite 1300, Chicago, IL 60605; 312–554–0166; www.apsac.org.
>
> Missing and Exploited Children's Training Programs, Fox Valley Technical College Criminal Justice Department, P.O. Box 2277, Appleton, WI 54913–2277; 800–648–4966; www.foxvalley.tec.wi.us/ojjdp.
>
> National Center for Prosecution of Child Abuse/American Prosecutors Research Institute, 99 Canal Center Plaza, Suite 510, Alexandria, VA 22314; 703–739–0321; www.ndaa-apri.org.
>
> National Center on Child Fatality Review, 4024 North Durfee Avenue, El Monte, CA 91732; 626–455–4585; www.ican-ncfr.org/.
>
> National Children's Alliance, 1319 F Street NW., Suite 1001, Washington, DC 20004; 800–239–9950 or 202–639–0597; www.nca-online.org.
>
> National Criminal Justice Reference Service (NCJRS), 2277 Research Boulevard, Rockville, MD 20850; 800–851–3420; www.ncjrs.org.

## Who's doing it?

A number of dependency court improvement initiatives are under way around the country. The following are two examples:

**Arizona Court Improvement Project.** Adopting the Model Dependency Court (referenced above, in Principle 3), Arizona has enacted legislation requiring juvenile courts to take a more active role in child welfare case oversight and decisionmaking. The legislation seeks to ensure safe and permanent homes for Arizona's children through comprehensive and timely judicial intervention.

T ragically, the systems that support children and families are too often the first to be cut when budgets are tight.

*For more information,* write The Honorable Nanette M. Warner, Presiding Judge, Pima County Juvenile Court Center, Division 20, 2225 East Ajo Way, Tucson, AZ 85713; or call 520–740–2054.

**Court reform efforts in New York City.** The New York City family courts have designed new court procedures to eliminate unnecessary delays and adjournments, reduce attorney scheduling conflicts, and increase the continuity of trials by forging stronger alliances with other agencies. Under the Family Justice Program, the court, in conjunction with various agencies, has initiated new procedures that can shorten the length of time a child is in foster care awaiting adoption or help a battered woman avoid the anxiety and frustration of unnecessary adjournments. In addition, a family court judge who had previously handled 20 different types of court proceedings can concentrate on just one area of family law and increase expertise in that area. Agencies that interact daily with the court also can dedicate personnel to the handling of specific types of cases. New York City's family court reforms also include the introduction of specialized domestic violence courts that seek to ensure continuity of court and agency personnel, intensive case monitoring, defendant accountability, and supportive services for victims. After 2 years, the Brooklyn Supreme Court Domestic Violence Court recorded significantly lower rates of dismissal, probation violation, and outstanding warrants.

*For more information,* write The Honorable Joseph M. Lauria, Administrative Judge, New York City Family Court, 60 Lafayette Street, New York, NY 10013; or call 212–374–3711.

(For additional action steps, see Principles 2 and 3.)

## Principle 6: Make adequate resources available

*We need to do this by dreaming big.*

—Ellen Cokinos, Executive Director, The Children's
Assessment Center, Halston, TX

The need for adequate resources is a constant refrain in human services, the criminal justice and healthcare systems, communities, and families. The story is the same when it comes to preventing and reducing the impact of children's exposure to violence: needs seem to exceed resources. Tragically, the systems that support children and families are too often the first to be cut when budgets are tight.

Resources are desperately needed for both prevention and intervention. Public expenditures on child welfare services far exceed expenditures on support and prevention programs such as Head Start and Early Head Start; childcare; the Women, Infants and Children's Supplemental Nutrition Program (WIC); and school lunch and breakfast programs.[48] In addition to prevention, there are other areas of particularly critical need, including funding to:

- Bring community partners to the table and build their capacity to collaborate in ways that enhance their community's response to children's exposure to domestic and other violence.

- Reduce caseloads and make needed resources available for child protection services and other direct service providers.

- Support and evaluate the effectiveness of offender rehabilitation programs that are part of a graduated range of sanctions that uses the coercive power of the criminal justice system to hold offenders accountable for their criminal acts of violence and for changing their behavior.

- Serve battered women who are seeking to create safety for themselves and their children (e.g., by meeting their need for housing, transportation, childcare, job training, etc.).

- Offer a full range of therapeutic treatments needed by children exposed to violence and training in practices that are sensitive to the developmental needs of children.

> *Legislation is passed all the time telling courts what they're supposed to do, but there is never any help to go along with it— no money for support staff, or to build a child-friendly courtroom. Without resources we are not enabling the judiciary to deal with this issue.*
>
> —The Honorable Ernestine Gray, Administrative Judge, Orleans Parish Juvenile Court

There is no doubt that addressing the needs of children exposed to violence is initially expensive. Yet over the long term, these expenditures prove to be extremely cost effective. Being abused or neglected as a child increases the likelihood of arrest as a juvenile by 53 percent and of arrest for a violent crime as an adult by 38 percent.[49] Therefore, preventing the violence or reducing its impact soon after it occurs means—at a minimum—saving the later costs of investigating, prosecuting, and rehabilitating juvenile and adult offenders who were child victims.

Some prevention programs that have studied expenditures versus outcomes are confirming the cost effectiveness of early, high-quality efforts. For example, the Tender Loving Care Home Visitation program in Oakland, CA, documents that the cost of the program in governmental and societal services ($6,000 per family per year) is recovered by the newborn child's fourth birthday and the projected cost savings over a child's lifetime are four times the cost of the program.

## Take action!

Making sure adequate resources are available to address children's exposure to violence means making better use of what is currently available (by improving coordination and encouraging volunteerism) and securing substantial and sustained financial investments—both public and private—in families, communities, and the systems that support and protect them.

There is no doubt that addressing the needs of children exposed to violence is initially expensive. Yet over the long term, these expenditures prove to be extremely cost effective.

T he California Children and Families Initiative (Proposition 10) levies a cigarette tax to be used to create a comprehensive, integrated program of early childhood development services.

The following are ways to make creative use of what is already available:

- **Community-based service agencies** can be the recipients of restitution checks from sex offenders or batterers. (Although individual amounts are small, they can add up.)

- **Governments** at the Federal, State, and local levels can review the range of funding streams available for children exposed to violence and, where possible, identify opportunities to improve the coordination of funding. Legislatures can create new funding mechanisms (see examples below, under "Who's doing it?"). Resources can be structured to be consistent with the principles in this Action Plan.

- **Healthcare professions** can take advantage of telemedicine (delivery of health services via telecommunication) to assist children who have been the victims of violence. This technique helps resolve access issues and allows a team approach to be implemented at lower cost and without retraumatizing the child.

- **Universities** can cover the costs of some of the training described in this Action Plan by incorporating training into existing curriculums and opening classes to professionals from the community.

## Who's doing it?

The following are examples of how to secure additional resources:

**California's Proposition 10.** The California Children and Families Initiative (Proposition 10) was passed by voters in November 1998. The Initiative levies a 50-cent-per-pack cigarette tax to be used to create, on a county-by-county basis, a comprehensive, integrated program of early childhood development services: health care, quality childcare, parent education, and intervention programs for families at risk.

*For more information on Proposition 10,* write California Children and Families Commission, 501 J Street, Suite 530, Sacramento, CA 95814; call 916–323–0056; e-mail info@ccfc.ca.gov; or visit www.ccfc.ca.gov.

**The Children's Board of Hillsborough County (Florida).** The Children's Board is a special taxing district for children's services. Legislation passed in Florida in the 1980's authorizes counties to take to public referendum the opportunity to assess property worth up to $5 million and use the funds for prevention and early intervention programs for children at the county level. In addition to standard child abuse prevention activities, services include childcare, media advocacy, comprehensive health care, research, and parent education.

*For more information,* write the Children's Board of Hillsborough County, 1205 East Eighth Avenue, Tampa, FL 33605–3503; call 813–229–2884; or visit www.childrensboard.org.

**Smart Start for Alaska's Children.** Smart Start is a comprehensive, inter-disciplinary plan to protect children, invest in proven prevention programs to break the cycle of family violence, and save money by reducing the costs associated with crime, health care, and welfare. Smart Start costs $32 million ($7 million for health care for 11,600 children and 800 pregnant women, $11 million for prevention programs, and $14 million for child protection programs) but does not require an increase in the State budget. Federal Medicaid payments to the State provide $31 million, and the remaining $1 million comes from higher taxes on snuff and chewing tobacco.

*For more information,* write Shari Paul, Office of the Governor, State of Alaska, P.O. Box 110001, Juneau, AK 99811; call 907–465–4870; or visit www.gov.state.ak.us/smartstart/index.htm.

**Victim Compensation in Santa Clara County (California).** California's comprehensive victim and witness assistance programs may be operated locally by government or by private nonprofit agencies. A program operates in every county of the State. In Santa Clara County, the National Conference for Community and Justice (NCCJ), a nonprofit human relations agency, has developed a number of strategies for aggressively seeking compensation for children who have been exposed to violence. (In California, children who have witnessed domestic violence are eligible for State compensation.) NCCJ places staff at the local Department of Social Services and family court and, through these sites alone, makes compensation claims for approximately 120 children each month. Each child receives up to $10,000 in mental health care. Under a new law, victims of domestic violence are now also eligible for compensation for relocation and home security expenses.

*For more information,* write Joe Yomtov, Director, Victim Witness Program, 777 North First Street, Suite 220, San Jose, CA 95112; call 408–295–2656; or visit www.victim.org.

In Santa Clara County, the National Conference for Community and Justice has developed a number of strategies for aggressively seeking compensation for children who have been exposed to violence.

# Principle 7: Work from a sound knowledge base

*We are talking about a lot of children. 8,000 in Miami, 31,500 in Chicago, 2,300 in Salt Lake City. Almost 500,000 children nationwide—1 to 2 percent of the children in every community. And we know so little about them . . . .*

—The Honorable Cindy Lederman,
Presiding Judge of the Miami-Dade Juvenile Court

*There's harder science that can be brought to bear. We must know with precision how much child abuse there is and whether it is rising or falling.*

—David Chadwick, MD,
Director Emeritus of the Center for Child Protection,
Children's Hospital, San Diego, CA

**W**herever possible, efforts to prevent and reduce the impact of children's exposure to violence must be based on solid research.

There are significant differences in philosophy, strategy, and focus among the diverse professionals working with children exposed to violence. Yet there is consensus that despite a strong foundation, much more solid research and data are needed. There is also consensus that this lack of information makes it difficult to select the most effective interventions and get them funded.

A number of areas of research and evaluation need particular attention, including:

■ Basic research on child development and resiliency.

■ Short- and long-term evaluations of a range of interventions, including child abuse and neglect interventions, efforts to rehabilitate offenders, school-based interventions, domestic violence advocacy, and others.

■ Research on the effectiveness of coordinated community response efforts.

■ Research that focuses on protective factors unique to particular communities and that assesses the impact of cultural competence in working with families. More information is also needed about systemic issues related to the overrepresentation of particular minority groups among victims and offenders, including patterns in case identification and selection.

## Take action!

Wherever possible, efforts to prevent and reduce the impact of children's exposure to violence must be based on solid research. These efforts must also be documented and evaluated so that future endeavors can be improved on the basis of experience. These imperatives are at the root of elevating the issue of children and violence to a level of national prominence, securing adequate funding, and, most important, protecting children and their families. Participants in the National Summit on Children Exposed to Violence identified three critical components of an effective research strategy:

■ Research should seek input from community members, practitioners, and victims and, where possible, should be conducted in active collaboration with them.

■ International collaboration should be fostered to gain and share knowledge worldwide.

■ More concerted efforts are needed to broadly disseminate research findings, best and promising practices, and community directories of resources and practices. Consideration should be given to establishing a national clearinghouse.

In 1994, recognizing the need for a greater synthesis of existing research in the area of violence prevention and intervention, the Institute of Medicine and the Board on Children, Youth and Families of the Commission on Behavioral and Social Sciences and Education of the National Research Council established a

Committee on the Assessment of Family Violence Interventions. The Committee has recently issued a series of reports examining the emerging social science research base on violence and families. (*For copies of reports,* call the National Academy Press at 800–624–6242 or visit www.nap.edu.)

---

## Additional resources for Principle 7: Work from a sound knowledge base

**For more information on available data and program resources, contact:**

American Humane Association, 63 Inverness Drive East, Englewood, CO 80112; 303–792–9900; www.americanhumane.org.

Crimes Against Children Research Center, University of New Hampshire, Horton Social Science Center, 20 College Road, Room 126, Durham, NH 03824; 603–862–1888; www.unh.edu/ccrc.

National Center for Juvenile Justice (the research arm of the National Council of Juvenile and Family Court Judges), 710 Fifth Avenue, Suite 3000, Pittsburgh, PA 15219; 412–227–6950; www ncjj.org.

National Clearinghouse on Child Abuse and Neglect Information, 330 C Street SW., Washington, DC 20447; 800–FYI (394)–3366 or 703–385–7565; www.calib.com/nccanch.

National Resource Center for Safe Schools, Northeast Regional Educational Laboratory, 101 Southwest Main Street, Suite 500, Portland, OR 97204; 800–268–2275; www nwrel.org/safe.

National Resource Center on Domestic Violence, 600 Flank Drive, Suite 1300, Harrisburg, PA 17112; 800–537–2238.

Resource Center on Domestic Violence: Child Protection and Custody, National Council of Juvenile and Family Court Judges, Family Violence Department, P.O. Box 8970, Reno, NV 89507; 800–527–3223; www nationalcouncilfvd.org.

**For additional coverage of this topic, see:**

"Convening a National Call to Action: Working Toward the Elimination of Child Maltreatment," *Child Abuse & Neglect The International Journal,* Special issue, 23(10), 1999.

A culture of nonviolence that supports children, women, and families is the vital context to ensure success.

# Principle 8: Create a culture of nonviolence

*We have to pull the fabric of community back around the children who have suffered so much.*

—Janet Reno, Attorney General of the United States

Each of the steps identified in this Action Plan has value for preventing and reducing the impact of children's exposure to violence. Taken together, these action steps will have even greater force. The greatest success, however, will be achieved when these actions are taken within a larger social environment that can help sustain them. A culture of nonviolence that supports children, women, and families is the vital context to ensure success.

In the broadest terms, this means creating a culture with zero tolerance for violence—one that promotes peaceful conflict resolution; rejects the use of power and control over children, women, and minorities; and respects racial, cultural, and class differences. It is also a culture that values and supports caregiving and parenting and recognizes the importance of the relationships between children and their parents and other caregivers, especially in the early years.

## Protective factors, collective efficacy, and children exposed to violence

This kind of culture would, of course, be desirable under any circumstances. But it would have particular significance for preventing and reducing the impact of children's exposure to violence. New studies are revealing two important facts. First, it has been demonstrated that the presence of "protective factors" (e.g., strong family relationships, alternative supports, dedicated daily time for children with a single caregiver, high expectations and a sense of purpose for children, and meaningful involvement in duties and community service, among others) can, in effect, guard children against the negative effects of exposure to violence.[50] Second, it has been demonstrated that when all other variables are eliminated, the one characteristic that accounts for less violence in a community is the willingness of neighbors to intervene on behalf of others. This "collective efficacy" is the neighborhoodwide determination of residents to stop violence or flag its possible precursors.[51]

There is evidence to suggest, then, that a culture supportive of families, women, and children would inherently provide the protective factors and the collective efficacy needed to keep children safe from violence. Many believe in the value of such primary prevention, but specific skills and training are needed to develop effective primary prevention strategies and initiatives.

## Take action!

There is no doubt that cultural change is a tall order. But there are a number of critical steps that agencies, communities, and individuals can take to achieve this goal.

**Agencies** can take the following steps:

■ **Ensure meaningful citizen involvement.** Agencies can build local leadership and capacity by involving parents and youth as real partners, especially in formulating policies and procedures. Agencies can also work with families to establish informal prevention and support networks in the community (e.g., kinship networks, mentoring programs, and self-help groups). These networks will extend the reach and effectiveness of the agency.

■ **Bring new voices to the table.** The interests, needs, and concerns of communities of color, immigrant and migrant communities, youth, and others are largely ignored as agencies and others make decisions about their goals and operating strategies. Without representation of diverse voices, the Nation will never overcome racism, sexism, and other roots of violence in society, specifically against children. Local and Federal agencies should mandate that decisionmaking bodies include voices that are often unheard.

■ **Use the bully pulpit.** Agency heads, judges, doctors, elected officials (prosecutors, county commissioners, city council members, and legislators), faith leaders, and others can be leaders in building community coalitions to take on the issues outlined below.

**Communities and individuals** can take the following steps:

■ **Focus on creating safe spaces.** Rebuilding the physical infrastructure of communities—the natural environment, play areas, transportation, facilities for community meetings and entertainment, schools, and shelters—is an important part of creating a culture of nonviolence that supports children, women, and families.

■ **Increase awareness about children's exposure to violence.** As noted earlier in this Action Plan, the public's understanding of the issue of children's exposure to violence is limited. Because it has been variously—and unsuccessfully—regarded as a health, education, welfare, or justice problem, it lacks a unified voice. As a result, there is a great need to have something to organize around and something toward which greater resources can be directed. Communities can take a number of steps to increase local awareness or to support broader national efforts, including developing public information campaigns.

■ **Stop gun violence.** Clearly, guns and other weapons play a role in the violence to which children, women, and families are exposed. Taking whatever steps are appropriate in a given community to stop gun violence is important.

■ **Hold the media accountable.** Communities can hold the media accountable for playing both positive and negative roles in children's exposure to

R ebuilding the physical infrastructure of communities is an important part of creating a culture of nonviolence that supports children, women, and families.

**T**he media should help ensure that efforts to educate parents and youth about violence include information about the roles and responsibilities of the media.

violence. Communities can seek to ensure that local news stations do not cover violence gratuitously, that local newspapers publish program ratings so parents can keep violent images out of their homes, and that the media report on positive efforts to stop violence, enhance protective factors, and implement collective efficacy. Communities and individuals can work with the media to develop compelling, accurate portrayals of the impact of violence on children. Representatives of the media should be included on community task forces and collaborative teams formed to address these issues. In addition, the media should participate in developing a range of tools (such as parental warnings and "V-chip" technology) to reduce children's exposure to violence over the airwaves. Finally, the media should help ensure that efforts to educate parents and youth about violence include information about the roles and responsibilities of the media.

> *We do a terrible job of covering child abuse because there is a thicket of difficulty in covering it accurately. So it takes a great deal of patience and belief in the story on the part of editors to make this work. We have to invest resources in these stories.*
>
> —Bob Levey, Columnist,
> *The Washington Post*

■ **Support community policing.** Neighborhoods that have community policing describe it as a foundation for problem-solving partnerships between communities and law enforcement. Through this strategy, law enforcement can also reorganize and reallocate resources to take a more holistic approach to working with families. In New Haven, CT, for example, the police department changed its Juvenile Division to the Family Services Unit to better serve families as a whole.

## Who's doing it?

**Boston's Problem-Solving Project.** Like other major cities, Boston, MA, has been grappling with the problem of youth, gang, and firearm violence. A National Institute of Justice-sponsored Problem-Solving Project has used innovative methods and a team approach to disrupt firearms markets and deter youth violence. The team—which includes Harvard University researchers, city-employed gang outreach and mediation specialists, and representatives of the Boston police, Federal Bureau of Alcohol, Tobacco and Firearms, U.S. Attorney's Office, Suffolk County District Attorney's Office, and Massachusetts Department of Probation— has developed real strategies for presenting gang members in Boston with a choice: "stop the flow of guns and stop the violence—or face rapid, focused, and comprehensive enforcement and corrections." Although it is too soon to evaluate the long-term effectiveness of the program, the immediate results have been very encouraging.

*For more information,* write David M. Kennedy, Senior Research Analyst, Kennedy School of Government, Harvard University, 79 John F. Kennedy Street, Cambridge, MA 02138 (or call 616–495–7533); or write Lieutenant Kevin Foley, Youth Violence Strike Force, Boston Police Department, 364 Warren Street, Roxbury, MA 02119 (or call 617–343–4444).

**The Child Wire.** A recently launched news service, The Child Wire expects to become the definitive source of news pertaining to and affecting children and the premier medium for positive, solution-oriented news stories about young people. The Child Wire concept was developed to create a newsroom atmosphere in which children's issues are met with seriousness and considered both news and newsworthy. Child Wire journalists will provide indepth reporting on broad topics that affect the growth and development of children.

*For more information,* write Rachel Jones, Founder and Chief Executive Officer, The Child Wire, P.O. Box 15575, Washington, DC 20003–0575; call 202–543–5033; or e-mail Rachella35@aol.com.

**Families and Schools Together (FAST).** This program model is dedicated to early intervention to help at-risk youth succeed. It offers youth structured opportunities for building relationships with parents and other family members, peers, other families, school representatives, and community members. The goal is to provide youth with a social safety net of protective factors to help them through difficult times. FAST has been widely acclaimed and replicated. The first 10 FAST trainers were certified in 1989; now, more than 250 trainers are active in the United States, Canada, and Australia.

*For more information,* write Lynn McDonald, Wisconsin Center for Education Research, University of Wisconsin-Madison, 1025 West Johnson, Madison, WI 53706; call 608–263–9476 or 608–663–2382; or visit www.wcer.wisc.edu/fast.

**Parents Anonymous, Inc.** The oldest national child abuse prevention organization in the United States, Parents Anonymous, Inc., is dedicated to strengthening families through mutual support and parent leadership. Parents Anonymous, Inc., leads a national network of affiliated community-based Parents Anonymous® groups that hold weekly meetings for approximately 100,000 parents and children around the country. These groups are led by parents and professionally trained facilitators. Many State and local programs operate telephone hotlines. In addition, Parents Anonymous, Inc., works to raise awareness and educate the public on critical issues and community- and policy-based solutions. Volunteers make up the core support for the programs.

*For more information,* write Parents Anonymous, Inc., 675 West Foothill Boulevard, Suite 220, Claremont, CA 91711; call 909–621–6184; e-mail parentsanon@msn.com; or visit www.parentsanonymous-natl.org.

P arents Anonymous, Inc., is dedicated to strengthening families through mutual support and parent leadership.

**R**isk-focused policing has transformed the police mission from one of simply apprehending criminals to one of controlling crime before it happens.

**Partnerships for Preventing Violence.** This free, national satellite broadcast training program specifically teaches violence prevention practitioners (not the lay public) how to implement effective primary prevention initiatives. The program is cosponsored by the U.S. Departments of Justice, Education, and Health and Human Services and is operated by the Prevention Institute.

*For more information,* write Rachel Davis, Prevention Institute, 1181 Colusa Avenue, Berkeley, CA 94707; call 510–528–4482; or visit www.walcoff.com/partnerships.

**Risk-focused policing.** The City of Redlands, CA, has transformed its paradigm for addressing neighborhood quality-of-life issues by consolidating housing, recreation, and senior services into the police department under the auspices of Risk- and Protective-Focused Prevention (RPFP). The RPFP program was adapted from an adolescent problem-prevention model developed by researchers at the University of Washington. Redlands' RPFP policing works to understand and address the causes and prevention of problems in adolescents—substance abuse, delinquency, violence, dropping out of school, and pregnancy—by transforming the police mission from one of simply apprehending criminals to one of controlling crime before it happens. Redlands has mapped community, family, school, and peer group risk and protective factors at the neighborhood level, enabling the police department and the many community-based organizations that share access to these data to effectively focus their limited resources.

*For more information,* write Chief Jim Bueermann, 212 Brookside Avenue, P.O. Box 1025, Redlands, CA 92373; or call 909–798–7661.

**Safe Schools/Healthy Students Initiative.** In 1999, the U.S. Departments of Education, Health and Human Services, and Justice launched the Safe Schools/Healthy Students Initiative to support comprehensive, integrated, communitywide approaches to promoting healthy childhood development and addressing the problems of school violence and alcohol and other drug abuse. Local initiatives will work from strategic plans that include issues such as school safety, violence and substance abuse prevention and treatment, school- and community-based mental health services for prevention and treatment, early childhood development, and educational reform. Grants totaling more than $141 million have been awarded to 77 communities to support implementation of 3-year projects.

*For more information,* write Kellie J. Dressler, Program Coordinator, U.S. Department of Justice, Office of Justice Programs, Office of Juvenile Justice and Delinquency Prevention, 800 K Street NW., Suite 300, Washington, DC 20531; call 202–514–4817; or e-mail dresslek@ojp.usdoj.gov.

# In Conclusion . . .

*When I had everything inside there was a lot of pressure on me.*
*When I let everything out I just felt relieved.*

—16-year-old girl

Children's exposure to violence is an issue that touches everyone—an American tragedy that scars children and threatens the safety of communities. A great challenge lies ahead: to help move this country closer to the day when children are no longer victims of and witnesses to violence, when they are given the support they need to thrive, and when they respond to conflict nonviolently, without destroying their lives and the lives of others. Taking the steps in this Action Plan will bring significant progress in this journey.

> **C**hildren's exposure to violence is an issue that touches everyone.

# Endnotes

1. Although it is recognized that men are sometimes battered, in approximately 95 percent of domestic violence cases, the victim is a woman (National Council of Juvenile and Family Court Judges, *Effective Intervention in Domestic Violence and Child Maltreatment Cases: Guidelines for Policy and Practice*, Reno, NV: National Council of Juvenile and Family Court Judges, 1999). In keeping with these data, and for the purposes of this document, domestic violence is assumed to refer to violence perpetrated by men against women in the context of an intimate relationship.

2. Many have enumerated the challenges in fully understanding and addressing children's exposure to violence. In 1998, for example, Children's Hospital and Health Center in San Diego, CA, began the process of developing its National Call to Action: Working Toward the Elimination of Child Maltreatment initiative. Among other things, this effort has further identified and delineated many of the challenges facing a national effort to eliminate child maltreatment. For more information, call the Children's Hospital and Health Center project at 858–495–4972.

3. D. Kilpatrick and B. Saunders, *Prevalence and Consequences of Child Victimization: Results from the National Survey of Adolescents, Final Report.* Research in Brief, Washington, DC: U.S. Department of Justice, Office of Justice Programs, National Institute of Justice, 1997, NCJ 181028 (for availability information, see p. x).

4. Kilpatrick and Saunders, 1997.

5. H.N. Snyder and M. Sickmund, *Juvenile Offenders and Victims: 1999 National Report*, Washington, DC: U.S. Department of Justice, Office of Justice Programs, Office of Juvenile Justice and Delinquency Prevention, 1999, NCJ 178257 (for availability information, see p. x).

6. U.S. Department of Health and Human Services, Administration on Children, Youth and Families, *Child Maltreatment 1997: Reports from the States to the National Child Abuse and Neglect Data System,* Washington, DC: U.S. Government Printing Office, 1997.

7. A.C. Huston, F. Donnerstine, H. Fairchild, N.D. Feshbach, P.A. Katz, J.P. Murray, E.A. Rubinstein, B.L. Wilcox, and D. Zuckerman, *Big World, Small Screen: The Role of Television in American Society.* Lincoln, NE: University of Nebraska Press, 1992.

8. U.S. Department of Justice, Office of Justice Programs, Office for Victims of Crime, *Breaking the Cycle of Violence: Recommendations To Improve the Criminal Justice Response to Child Victims and Witnesses,* Monograph, Washington, DC: U.S. Department of Justice, June 1999, NCJ 176983 (for availability information, see p. x).

9. L. Taylor, B. Zuckerman, V. Harik, and B.M. Groves, Witnessing violence by young children and their mothers, *Journal of Developmental and Behavioral Pediatrics* 15(2):120–123, 1994.

10. Taylor et al., 1994.

11. U.S. Department of Health and Human Services, Administration on Children, Youth and Families, 1997.

12. Snyder and Sickmund, 1999.

13. Snyder and Sickmund, 1999.

14. Kilpatrick and Saunders, 1997.

15. R.S. Pynoos and K. Nader, Children who witness the sexual assaults of their mothers, *Journal of the American Academy of Child and Adolescent Psychiatry* 27(5):567–572, 1988.

16. National Clearinghouse on Child Abuse and Neglect Information, *In Harm's Way: Domestic Violence and Child Maltreatment,* Washington, DC: National Clearinghouse on Child Abuse and Neglect Information, 1999, p.1.

17. U.S. Department of Justice, Office of Justice Programs, Office for Victims of Crime, June 1999.

18. U.S. Department of Health and Human Services, Administration on Children, Youth and Families, 1997.

19. M.A. Straus and R.J. Gelles, *Physical Violence in American Families: Risk Factors and Adaptations to Violence in 8145 Families,* New Brunswick, NJ: Transaction Publishers, 1990, pp. 553 (table B.1) and 555 (Table B.3).

20. C.S. Widom, *The Cycle of Violence,* Research in Brief, U.S. Department of Justice, Office of Justice Programs, National Institute of Justice, 1992, NCJ 136607 (for availability information, see p. x).

21. Widom, 1992.

22. Widom, 1992.

23. Kilpatrick and Saunders, 1997.

24. National Council of Juvenile and Family Court Judges, *Effective Intervention in Domestic Violence and Child Maltreatment Cases: Guidelines for Policy and Practice,* Reno, NV: National Council of Juvenile and Family Court Judges, 1999, p. 10.

25. U.S. Department of Justice, Office of Justice Programs, Office for Victims of Crime, June 1999.

26. U.S. Department of Justice, Office of Justice Programs, Office for Victims of Crime, June 1999.

27. For practical guidelines on interdisciplinary cooperation in the investigation of child abuse, see *Forming a Multidisciplinary Team To Investigate Child Abuse,* Portable Guides to Investigating Child Abuse, U.S. Department of Justice, Office of Justice Programs, Office of Juvenile Justice and Delinquency Prevention, 1998, NCJ 170020 (for availability information see p. x). This manual explains the benefits of a multidisciplinary team to investigate child abuse and provides advice on forming and operating an effective team.

28. For related information, see M.L. Medaris, E. Campbell, and B. James, *Sharing Information: A Guide to the Family Educational Rights and Privacy Act and Participation in Juvenile Justice Programs,* U.S. Department of Justice, Office of Justice Programs, Office of Juvenile Justice and Delinquency Prevention and U.S. Department of Education, Family Policy Compliance Office, June 1997, NCJ 163705 (for availability information, see p. x).

29. Medaris, Campbell, and James, 1997.

30. D.J. Siegel, *The Developing Mind: Toward a Neurobiology of Interpersonal Experience,* New York: The Guilford Press, 1999, p. 13.

31. Taylor et al., 1994.

32. U.S. Department of Health and Human Services, Administration on Children, Youth and Families, 1997.

33. U.S. Department of Health and Human Services, Administration on Children, Youth and Families, 1997.

34. J. McFarlane, B. Parker, and K. Soekan, Abuse during pregnancy: Associations with maternal health and infant birth weight, *Nursing Research* 45(1):37–42, 1996.

35. C.C. Bell, S. Gamm, P. Vallas, and P. Jackson, Strategies for the prevention of youth violence in Chicago public schools, in *School Violence: Contributing Factors, Management and Prevention,* edited by M. Shafi and S. Shafi, Washington, DC: American Psychiatric Press, in press.

36. For related information, see D. Olds, P. Hill, and E. Rumsey, *Prenatal and Early Childhood Nurse Home Visitation,* Bulletin, U.S. Department of Justice, Office of Justice Programs, Office of Juvenile Justice and Delinquency Prevention, November 1998, NCJ 172875 (for availability information, see p. x).

37. OJJDP is currently funding a demonstration and evaluation of nurse home visitation in six sites.

38. U.S. Department of Justice, Office of Justice Programs, Office for Victims of Crime, June 1999.

39. For related information, see J. McNaughton, *Overview of the Portable Guides to Investigating Child Abuse: Update 2000,* Bulletin, U.S. Department of Justice, Office of Justice Programs, Office of Juvenile Justice and Delinquency Prevention, February 2000, NCJ 178893 (for availability information, see p. x).

40. Kilpatrick and Saunders, 1997.

41. National Clearinghouse on Child Abuse and Neglect Information, 1999, p. 2.

42. U.S. Department of Justice, Office of Justice Programs, Office for Victims of Crime, June 1999.

43. National Council of Juvenile and Family Court Judges, 1999, based on research reported by J.S. Edelson, Children's witnessing of adult domestic violence, *Journal of Interpersonal Violence* 14(8):839–870, 1999. Also see S. Schecter and J.S. Edelson, *Domestic Violence and Children: Creating a Public Response,* New York, NY: Center on Crime, Communities & Culture of the Open Society Institute, 2000.

44. Schecter and Edelson, 2000.

45. Schecter and Edelson, 2000.

46. Schecter and Edelson, 2000.

47. Schecter and Edelson, 2000, pp. 109–110.

48. M. Courtney, The economics, paper presented at the San Diego Conference on Responding to Child Maltreatment, January 26, 1999.

49. Widom, 1992.

50. Notes of Summit participant Domonique Hensler, Community Health Administrator, Children's Hospital and Health Center, San Diego, CA.

51. R.J. Sampson, S.W. Raudenbush, and F. Earls, Neighborhoods and violent crime: A multilevel study of collective efficacy, *Science* 277:918–924, 1997.